Contents

LEAAM

14-19 Education and Skills

**Presented to Parliament by
the Secretary of State for Education and Skills
by Command of Her Majesty**

February 200

Cm 6476

£19.25

Foreword
by the Secretary of State
for Education and Skills

I am proud that my first White Paper as Secretary of State should be on the issue of education for our 14 to 19 year-olds.

The reforms I set out here are of vital importance. They are vital to our economy – equipping young people with the skills employers need and the ability to go on learning throughout their lives. They are vital for social justice – giving us the chance to break forever the historic link between social background, educational achievement and life chances that have dogged us as a nation. And most of all they are vital to each and every individual young person, whatever their needs and whatever their aspirations.

Today's teenagers are tomorrow's parents, entrepreneurs, public servants and community leaders. So the stakes could not be higher. I believe that every child and every teenager has equal worth. We owe it to them to give them the chance to show what they can do, to make the most of their talents, to reach their potential. And the key to doing that is to design a system around them – based on high standards, on choice and on meeting individuals' needs and aspirations.

To deliver that system will take determination. It will take commitment. It will take the hard work of teachers, lecturers, other education professionals, employers, parents and all who work in or with our schools and colleges. It will require breaking down the artificial barriers between academic and vocational education. It will mean building on all that is good in our system and reforming what is not working.

The White Paper sets out the detail of our reform programme, building from the excellent work of Sir Mike Tomlinson and his Working Group on 14-19 Reform and from the work of the successful school and college partnerships we are already seeing in local communities. It charts a 10-year reform programme and the milestones needed to achieve it. But more than those details and those milestones, it sets out a vision of what we want for children and teenagers – what we want them to learn, the skills we want them to acquire, but above all the values we want them to have.

The purpose of the education system is to help each and every individual reach their potential. This White Paper sets out how we will build a system of 14 to 19 education that will do just that. A system that we can be proud of. And one that gives every young person the opportunities they need and deserve.

Ruth Kelly

Ruth Kelly
Secretary of State for Education and Skills

Executive Summary

1. Our aim is to transform secondary and post-secondary education so that all young people achieve and continue in learning until at least the age of 18.

2. Since 1997, we have carried through far-reaching reforms to raise standards, made possible by substantial new investment in schools and colleges. Primary school standards are at their highest ever level – and in international comparisons, our primary schools match the best anywhere. Results at secondary school are also at their best ever level: in 2004, over 53% of young people achieved 5 or more A*-C grade GCSEs (or equivalent), compared to around 45% in 1997. We have also put in place a range of measures to tackle barriers to learning. Education Maintenance Allowances provide a strong incentive for 16-19 year-olds to stay in education and have a proven track record in increasing participation.

3. But the challenges ahead remain considerable. Numbers staying on post-16 have improved but are still too low – far down the international league table. Many employers are not satisfied with the basic skills of school leavers going directly into jobs. Some young people drift outside education, employment or training between the ages of 16 and 19. The most able young people are not as fully stretched as they could be.

4. We propose therefore a radical reform of the system of 14-19 education – curriculum, assessment and the range of opportunities on offer. The Working Group on 14-19 Reform, chaired by Sir Mike Tomlinson, reported in October last year. This White Paper is our response.

5. In it we set out our proposals for an education system focused on high standards and much more tailored to the talents and aspirations of individual young people, with greater flexibility about what and where to study and when to take qualifications. These proposals will:

- tackle our low post-16 participation – we want participation at age 17 to increase from 75% to 90% over the next 10 years;

- ensure that every young person has a sound grounding in the basics of English and maths and the skills they need for employment;

- provide better vocational routes which equip young people with the knowledge and skills they need for further learning and employment;

- stretch all young people; and

- re-engage the disaffected.

A strong foundation at Key Stage 3

6. Our first step is to make sure that Key Stage 3 – 11-14 education – provides a stronger base of knowledge and skills. By the age of 14, we want young people to have achieved higher standards in the basics and to have acquired a sound education – and an enthusiasm for learning – across the curriculum. That will be the platform for the increased choice teenagers will have between

the ages of 14 and 19. In order to achieve this, we will:

- retain all of the core and foundation subjects within that phase, but review the curriculum to improve its coherence in subjects where there are problems. We will reduce prescription so that schools have space to help those below the expected level to catch up and to stretch all their pupils;

- support and challenge schools through the Secondary National Strategy and the New Relationship with Schools to use the new flexibility well;

- strengthen the emphasis on English and maths, in particular by expecting schools to focus systematically on those who arrive from primary school without having reached the expected standard in the Key Stage 2 literacy and numeracy tests, continue to publish national test results and introduce a new on-line test of ICT skills;

- introduce models of moderated teacher assessment in the other compulsory subjects, providing professional development for teachers to support their skills in assessing young people, which will help to raise standards across the curriculum; and

- emphasise the importance of achievement at age 14 by recording in a 'Pupil Profile' for each young person and their parents, achievement across the curriculum.

7. By doing so, we will ensure that more young people achieve National Curriculum level 5 in English, maths, science and ICT; and that all young people are stretched to achieve across all subjects.

A strong core 14-19

8. Achieving functional skills in English and maths must be at the heart of the 14-19 phase. These skills are essential to support learning in other subjects and they are essential for employment. Achieving level 2 (GCSE level) in functional English and maths is a vital part of a good education. In order to ensure more young people achieve that grounding:

- we have already reduced the amount of prescription in the Key Stage 4 curriculum, providing more scope for schools to support catch-up in English and maths;

- we are extending the Key Stage 3 Strategy to improve classroom practice, so that it provides support across secondary schools;

- we will expect more teenagers to achieve 5 A*-C grade GCSEs including English and maths and we will introduce a general (GCSE) Diploma to recognise those who achieve this standard;

- we will toughen the GCSE Achievement and Attainment Tables, showing what percentage of young people have achieved the Diploma standard – ie 5 A*-C grade GCSEs including English and maths. We expect to phase out the existing 5 A*-C measure by 2008;

- we will ensure that no-one can get a C or better in English and maths without mastering the functional elements. Where a teenager achieves the functional element only, we will recognise that separately; and

- we will provide more opportunities and incentives for teenagers who have not achieved level 2 by 16 to do so post-16 and support them in achieving level 1 or entry level qualifications as steps on the way.

Routes to success for all

9. Building on that core, we will create a system better tailored to the needs of the individual pupil, in which teenagers are stretched to achieve. We will:

- introduce greater choice of what and where to study and make it easier to combine academic and vocational learning;

- retain GCSEs and A levels as cornerstones of the new system;

- introduce new specialised Diplomas, including academic and vocational material, covering each occupational sector of the economy. The Diplomas will be available at levels 1 (foundation), 2 (GCSE) and 3 (advanced);

- require that anyone achieving a Diploma at level 2 must have functional English and maths at level 2;

- put employers in the lead through Sector Skills Councils, in designing specialised Diplomas which provide the right grounding for work and further study, supported by higher education and the QCA; and

- challenge and support schools and colleges to ensure that young people take qualifications when they are ready, not at a fixed age, encouraging acceleration to level 2 and ensuring early achievement at advanced level is recognised in performance tables and elsewhere.

10. We understand and appreciate the argument that we should challenge our A level students further, by demanding more breadth. But there is no clear consensus amongst pupils, parents, employers or universities on whether and how it should be done. We also believe that so soon after the introduction of Curriculum 2000, stability is important. We will therefore work with employers and universities to see if we can identify what, if anything, would add value to existing courses and we will review progress in 2008. By this time we will also have the evidence from the pilots of the extended project and other measures to draw on.

A new system of specialised Diplomas

11. The Diplomas we are proposing will work as follows:

- To achieve a Diploma, young people will need to achieve appropriate standards in English and maths, specialised material, relevant GCSEs and A levels and have work experience.

- We will introduce the Diplomas in 14 lines and make these a national entitlement by 2015. The first four Diplomas in information and communication technology, engineering, health and social care and creative and media will be available in 2008. Eight will be available by 2010.

- We will work with employers to offer more opportunities to young people to learn at work and outside school.

- We will continue to improve the quality and number of employment-based training places through Apprenticeships, bringing them within the Diploma framework.

Strengthening GCSEs and A levels

12. We will keep both GCSEs and A levels, but improve both in those areas where there is a strong case for change. At GCSE we will:

- restructure English and maths GCSEs to make sure it is impossible to get a grade C or above without the ability to use functional English and maths;

- review coursework to reduce the assessment burden;

- continue work to reform maths as proposed by Professor Adrian Smith, improving motivation and progression to advanced level. This is likely to include a new double maths GCSE; and

- continue to promote science – including implementing the new science GCSEs – restating our firm expectation that young people should do two science GCSEs.

13. At A level we will:

- increase stretch for the most able by introducing optional harder questions into separate sections at the end of A level papers;

- introduce an 'extended project' to stretch all young people and test a wider range of higher-level skills;

- enable the most able teenagers to take HE modules while in the sixth form;

- ensure that universities have more information on which to make judgements about candidates by ensuring that they have access to the grades achieved by young people in individual modules by 2006. We will also support those universities who wish to have marks as well as grades; and

- we will reduce the assessment burden at A level by reducing the numbers of assessments in an A level from 6 to 4 but without reducing the standard or changing the overall content of A levels.

14. We will ensure that there are natural progression routes both through the levels of the Diploma and between GCSEs and A levels and the different levels of the Diploma. By doing so, we will secure for all teenagers routes that avoid early narrowing down, but provide real choice of what to learn and in what setting.

15. We believe that the current balance between internal and external assessment is essentially the right one to secure public confidence in the examinations system. We therefore do not propose major change here.

Engaging all young people

16. Our reforms will create opportunities for all young people. For many, the curriculum choices introduced in this White Paper will provide the opportunities they need to develop their talents and so succeed. The vocational opportunities, including different styles and places of learning, will motivate many. Foundation and entry level qualifications will help put more young people onto a pathway that will lead to further opportunities and qualifications.

17. For young people who face serious personal problems, the proposals in the Government's programme, 'Every Child Matters', will be crucial in breaking down the barriers to achievement. In addition, we will develop a pilot programme for 14-16 year-olds, based on the post-16 Entry to Employment programme. This new route will:

- provide a tailored programme for each young person and intensive personal guidance and support;

- involve significant work-based learning, probably amounting to two days each week;

- lead towards a level 1 Diploma; and

- lead on to a range of further options including Apprenticeship.

18. We expect this to be available to up to 10,000 young people from 2007/8.

A system configured around young people

19. We have designed these changes to the curriculum and qualifications to meet the needs of learners and employers. We will ensure that every part of the education system is configured to meet their needs.

20. We will increase the capacity of the education system to offer vocational education. We will do so by building on existing strengths – for example, extending the role of Centres of Vocational Excellence to making excellent vocational provision available for young people. We will also develop new Skills Academies as national centres of excellence in skills. We will strengthen schools' capacity to offer vocational education, through specialism. The best Specialist Schools will be able to become a leading school with additional resources to boost vocational provision. Significantly more post-16 opportunities will be needed to meet the objectives set out in this paper. Both schools and colleges will make additional provision. We will be consulting in detail on our proposals, set out in our 5-year plan, for a presumption in favour of high-performing 11-16 schools engaging in post-16 provision.

21. We will support the workforce to deliver. We will ensure that the right staff are in place, including those who have the necessary experience of the workplace to deliver vocational education, and that they have the professional development, qualifications and support that they need.

22. Schools, colleges and other providers will take the lead in each local area. A prospectus of options will be made available to all young people, setting out what is on offer to them.

Where there are any gaps, it will be the responsibility of local authorities and the local Learning and Skills Councils to commission provision to fill them. Each school and college will be expected to make the full range of choices available to young people on its roll, though perhaps at other institutions. Inspection will ensure that this is delivered.

An accountability framework which makes sure that we offer the best to young people

23. Finally, we need an accountability framework which supports and encourages the development of the new 14-19 phase. We will:

- include vocational qualifications in Achievement and Attainment Table measures and ensure that inspections challenge schools to offer the full range of curriculum and qualifications;

- focus on the basics through continuing to publish tables showing performance in English, maths and science at Key Stage 3; and toughening tables at 16 to measure the Diploma standard: 5 A*-C GCSEs including English and maths;

- encourage stretch for all teenagers through giving schools credit in the tables when they achieve success in higher level qualifications. Through the New Relationship with Schools, hold schools more strongly to account for the progress of all their students; and

- encourage institutions to focus on improving staying-on rates by introducing progression targets; and crediting schools for the achievement of young people completing Key Stage 4 later than the normal age.

24. This major package of reform seizes a once-in-a-generation chance to transform 14-19 education and skills. Through doing so, we will seek to widen opportunity for all young people and take the next steps towards a more prosperous and fairer society.

Chapter 1
Introduction

1.1. The transformation of secondary and post-secondary education, so that all 16 year-olds achieve highly and carry on into sixth form, college, an Apprenticeship or work with training until at least the age of 18, is a critical priority for Britain. It is central to building a more prosperous and fair society; and it is vital for the well-being and fulfilment of each individual young person in today's world.

1.2. Since 1997, we have carried through far-reaching reforms to raise standards in secondary and post-secondary education, made possible by substantial new investment in schools, colleges and training. We have the best ever results at primary level, at Key Stage 3, at GCSE and at A level. Particularly at primary level, schools in England are as good as those in any country. And we increasingly perform well in international comparisons up to age 16.

1.3. But the challenge ahead remains immense. Participation among 16-19 year olds remains very low by international standards. We are close to the bottom of the OECD league table for participation among 17 year-olds. That is now the burning problem facing our education service. The system for 14-19 education – curriculum, assessment and the range of opportunities on offer – needs radical modernisation to meet contemporary and future demands.

1.4. This White Paper sets out the Government's proposals to meet these challenges – seizing a once in a generation opportunity. We set out proposals which are designed to tackle the scandal of our low post-16 participation – we want to raise participation over a 10-year period from 75% to 90% at 17; to take a decisive step forward in vocational education; to secure the functional skills that all young people need for employment; to stretch all young people to succeed; and to re-engage the disaffected. Our proposals will deliver our twin aims of social justice and a competitive economy.

1.5. It is now four years since we first set out in 2001 our intention to reform education for 14-19 year-olds in our Green Paper 'Schools: Building on Success'. It is two years since we established a Working Group on 14-19 Reform under the expert chairmanship of Sir Mike Tomlinson. The Working Group has now produced an important report, setting out its proposals for change. This White Paper sets out the Government's plans for the 14-19 phase in England, responding to that report and moving us on to implement large-scale change.

1.6. In the last four years, there have been significant changes. It has become a normal part of life in schools in this country that some young people are studying and achieving recognised qualifications in vocational subjects before 16. New GCSEs in vocational subjects have been launched and the first group of young people have just succeeded in obtaining their qualifications. The Increased Flexibility Programme has given around 90,000 young people the opportunity to spend some time learning subjects in colleges which cannot easily be offered in schools. And from September 2004, for the first time, we have 14 year olds pursuing Young Apprenticeships, giving them the chance to combine school studies with learning alongside skilled workers. Work-related learning is now a statutory

requirement and the entitlement to enterprise education will be in place by September 2005.

1.7. In some parts of the country, designated as 14-19 pathfinder areas, the process has gone even further. Schools and colleges have worked with local authorities and the Learning and Skills Council (LSC) to offer young people a range of options which goes beyond what any one institution can provide and which is succeeding in attracting many more young people to learning. In other places, new sixth forms and colleges are being opened, boosting participation and choice.

1.8. Over the same period, and alongside developing and testing new models, we have consulted very widely on the long-term changes that we will need. The Working Group's work too has involved them in extensive and detailed discussions with the full range of interested parties. The consultation has involved young people and parents, industry and employers, higher education, schools and colleges, and a very wide range of representative bodies and interests.

1.9. This is the context of this White Paper. It is one in which the case for change is widely recognised and in which change is already underway. And it is common ground that reform should be pursued urgently in the interests of this generation of young people.

The purpose of the White Paper

1.10. Our task here is to set a long-term course and to chart the steps that will be needed to follow that course. We are firm in our convictions about the need for change; and

clear about the things that need to be done now. In making these the priorities for immediate action, we are also clear that we must not overburden the system with change. So we will move swiftly on the priorities as part of a longer-term programme of reform. The proposals in this White Paper, together with the forthcoming Skills White Paper, address our aim of equipping young people and adults with the skills they need to be employable and to achieve success later in life. The two White Papers offer employers the opportunity to contribute to the long-term transformation of vocational education in support of a high productivity, flexible economy.

1.11. In setting out our long-term course, we send a clear signal that our intention is that the system should be fashioned around the needs of the learner and be responsive to the needs of employers. The job of educational institutions is to ensure, locality by locality, that the full range of programmes is made available to young people.

1.12. We do not seek to prescribe every step that will be made to achieve our ambitions. Given the variety of local circumstances, the changing nature of society and the economy and the ongoing development of technologies that support learning, to do so would be foolish. However, it is as much the job of this White Paper to set out the changes in organisation and incentives that will secure delivery as to set out the changes in curriculum and qualifications that will improve what is available to young people.

1.13. Our starting point is to make clear the issues that need to be resolved.

1.14. This White Paper is concerned with England only, though we recognise that a number of our proposals have implications for Wales, Northern Ireland and, to a lesser extent, Scotland, especially where shared qualifications will be affected. In implementing our proposals, we will work closely with colleagues in those countries. In particular, when we are asking QCA to undertake work, we shall ask them to do so in co-operation with their fellow regulatory authorities to ensure that developments take account of the needs and circumstances in other parts of the UK and are compatible with structures there. The plans in this White Paper will be financed within available resources over the 2004 spending review period. Future resources will be determined in the normal way.

Chapter 2
The challenges we must overcome

Summary

Standards have risen significantly over recent years at all levels of the education system. Equally, the demand for higher-level skills in the economy continues to grow, and there are more jobs requiring high level skills. The costs to individuals, the economy and society of educational failure are high. We agree with the Working Group on 14-19 Reform's analysis of these challenges.

More young people achieve well at school. In 2004, over 53% of young people achieved 5 or more A*-C grade GCSEs, compared to around 45% in 1997. Compared to other countries, standards by the age of 16 are good, but staying on rates after the age of 16 poor. Consequently, the proportion of the population having skills at level 2 (intermediate) or level 3 (advanced) is lower than in other advanced industrial countries. The biggest gap is in the achievement of vocational qualifications. Employers are also concerned about the basic skills of those school leavers moving directly into employment.

The confusing array of qualifications and the existing curriculum contribute to the problems. Not all qualifications offer good progression routes to higher levels. The lack of widespread recognition of many of them contributes to the perception that they are second rate. GCSEs and A levels are well understood, but there has been increasing concern that they need strengthening both to stretch the most able and to provide better progression. Furthermore, the current system in which most young people take all their qualifications at fixed ages is not well tailored to the varied talents and aptitudes of young people.

2.1. There has been very significant progress in recent years in raising standards across the school system. International evidence now shows that our primary schools are world class on any measure. Improved results in literacy and numeracy are borne out in international survey evidence from PIRLS (Progress in International Reading Literacy Study) and TIMSS (Trends in International Mathematics and Science Study), which show our primary school children among the world leaders in English, maths and science. England ranked 3rd in PIRLS, 5th in science in TIMSS and was the most improved nation in maths (see Figure 2.1).

Figure 2.1: England's performance in TIMSS: 10 year-olds

	1995	2003
Grade 4 science		
Score	528	540
Ranking	8th out of 26	5th out of 25
Grade 4 maths		
Score	484	531
Ranking	17th out of 26	10th out of 25

Source: IEA's Trends in International Mathematics and Science Study at the Fourth and Eighth Grades.

2.2. Secondary education, too, is very significantly improved. Since 1997, GCSE results have risen, so that where then only 45% of young people got 5 or more GCSEs at grade C or above (or equivalent), now over 53% do. Test results for 14 year-olds and success rates in colleges are also up.

2.3. But there remain significant challenges. The changing context of work and society and the need for the UK to be economically competitive place increasing demands on the knowledge and skills of the population. Our levels of participation in post-compulsory education are well behind those of most similar countries. And vocational education has less impact on skills levels in this country than it does in others.

2.4. Inspection evidence shows that much post-16 provision is very good. But there is considerable variability of quality and so considerable variability in the success of learners. Since inspections began in 2001, 90% of provision in colleges and 61% in work-based learning providers has been judged to be satisfactory or better. Through the 'Success for All' reforms, we are putting in place measures that will significantly accelerate the improvements in quality over the next few years.

Economic and social change mean that the need for education and high-level skills is greater than ever before

2.5. In this interdependent world, currents of economic change in other parts of the world can quickly affect this country and technology increasingly means that even service industries serving one country can be sited in another. Changes in the traditional industrial base have already profoundly changed the nature of many of our communities. The availability of low-skill, manual jobs has declined over a long period and for most, physical strength alone is no longer a sufficient basis for employment.

2.6. The changes to our expectations of working life, too, have been profound. The modern world – in the labour market and beyond – makes greater demands on a young person's capacity to communicate, present themselves, work in teams and understand diversity. No longer is there an assumption that the sector in which a young person starts work is the one in which they will end their career. For most, movement between jobs is the norm; for many, movement between entirely different sectors of the economy a realistic prospect. Young people may also want to further their careers in other countries. We must expect that the ability to move successfully between jobs in this way will be a growing necessity for the young people of today over the course of their working lives.

2.7. In this context, the need to offer every young person the opportunity to become educated and skilled is not only an economic imperative, but a moral one. Young people who do not have a good grounding in the basics and the right skills and knowledge for employment will not have much prospect of making the most of themselves in life and at work. If young people leave full-time education without well-respected and recognised qualifications, then they are unlikely to be able

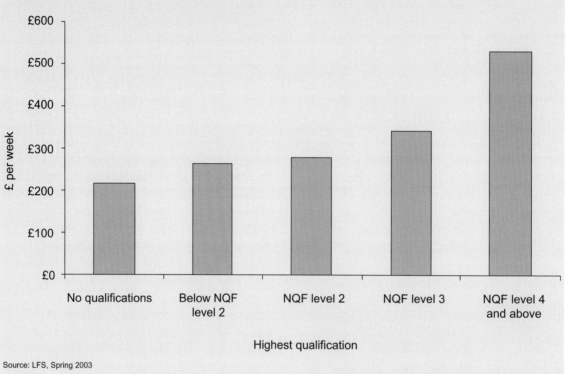

Figure 2.2: Education increases the productivity of the workforce, reflected in higher wages. Analysis of gross weekly earnings from the labour force survey show that earnings increase with qualification levels

Source: LFS, Spring 2003

to gain employment and then cope with the changing context of work through their lives. And the ongoing social and technological change that affects our world demands that more young people are prepared not only with transferable skills but also to adapt and learn throughout their lifetime. In simple financial terms, as Figure 2.2 shows, those who achieve higher levels of qualification will earn more.[1]

2.8. The wider economic need is significant too and the cost for all of us if we do not succeed, great. If we are to continue to attract many of the high value-added industries to this country, and to compete effectively on the global stage, then we will need far more of our population to have high levels of education. A critical mass of highly-skilled people will continue to attract those employers to this country. We also need

Figure 2.3: Correlation between offending behaviour and truancy

	Males		Females	
	12-16 %offender	17-30 %offender	12-16 %offender	17-30 %offender
Truant at least once a month	47	21	30	9
Occasional truant	13	16	18	3
No truant	10	8	4	2

Source: YLS 1998/9 HO RS 209 – note 12-16 year olds were asked about truanting in the last year. Those aged 17+ were asked about truanting in their last year of school

[1] Levels refer to National Qualifications Framework (NQF) levels. Level 2 is intermediate level (equivalent to 5 or more A*-C grade GCSEs); level 3 is advanced level (equivalent to 2 or more A levels); level 4 is equivalent to first degree level.

to ensure that our population is not making choices based on stereotypes, but on the basis of clear advice and guidance. The benefits of more engaging work, higher living standards and prosperity will flow to all of us.

2.9. Wider society's need for young people to achieve educational success goes beyond the needs of the economy, however. There is a strong and well-documented association between poor attendance and behaviour at school and later anti-social behaviour and criminality, as Figure 2.3 shows.

2.10. Tackling disengagement, truancy and poor behaviour at school are essential; providing motivating routes to success a necessity. It is in all our interests that we avoid the costs of failure to the individual and to wider society. And if we are to have a healthy society of responsible, active citizens, well-prepared to take a role in our democracy and the international community, then our education system provides us with the means of achieving that.

2.11. For all of these reasons, the need for an education system which offers high-quality routes to success for all young people has never been greater. For all the progress of recent years, there remain significant challenges to be overcome.

Though achievement at 15 has risen and compares well internationally, the staying on rate at 17 is poor

2.12. GCSE results have risen consistently over the last 15 years and should rise further as pupils who have benefited from reforms to primary education and Key Stage 3 reach age 16. It is easy to forget that the expectation before the introduction of GCSE was that the average student would gain a grade 4 CSE – equivalent to an F grade at GCSE. Many young people did not enter public examinations at all. That was a national scandal, sometimes referred to as our 'long tail of underachievement'. So although there has been consistent improvement in achievement

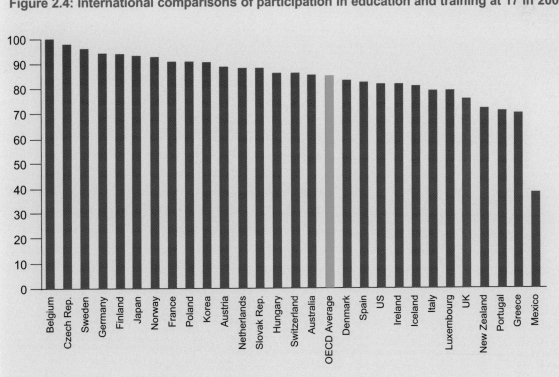

Figure 2.4: International comparisons of participation in education and training at 17 in 2002

Source: Organisation for Economic Co-operation and Development (2004) Education at a Glance: OECD Indicators 2004 Paris: OECD

since 1997, it has been against a background of deeply entrenched cultural expectations among many that some groups of young people would fail and leave learning at 16.

2.13. Key international comparisons published by the OECD confirm that we have relatively high standards at 15, but low staying on rates after 16 (Figure 2.4). In the last few years, as Figure 2.5 shows, rising attainment by age 16 has not been matched by rising participation post-16 (as it typically had been previously). This is not wholly negative, because it is partly the success of our economy and the very low level of youth unemployment in this country that makes the option of finding work attractive. But we would want many more young people to see it to be in their interests to continue in learning. And we must continue to reduce the number of young people who are not in employment, education or training (NEET).

2.14. As a result of low participation, skill levels in our workforce are behind those of other similar countries. This is because many fewer

people have vocational qualifications. It is important that we match other countries in maintaining education and training into young adulthood if we are to close the gap.

Young people who do not get 5 A*-C grade GCSEs (or equivalent) by age 16 do not have good opportunities to achieve success later

2.15. By far the best-known and best-understood qualifications for young people in this country are the GCSE and the A level. The overwhelming majority of young people who do well at GCSE level go on to take A level. However, even among those who get 5 A*-C GCSEs, a high proportion do not get English and maths. Those who succeed at A level often go on to university. Progression routes into further study for those who pursue other qualifications are much less clear.

2.16. Of course, there are concerns about even the well-established academic route. There are concerns about lack of breadth post-16 in the

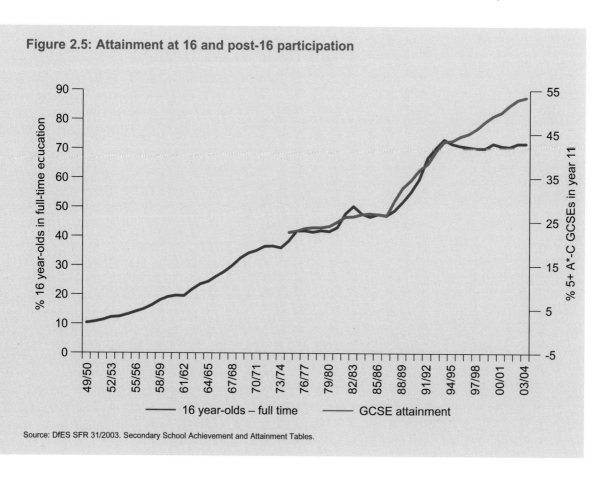

Figure 2.5: Attainment at 16 and post-16 participation

— 16 year-olds – full time   — GCSE attainment

Source: DfES SFR 31/2003. Secondary School Achievement and Attainment Tables.

A level programmes even of those who do get 5 A*-C grade GCSEs. There are concerns about the extent to which the most able are really stretched – with some young people acquiring large numbers of GCSEs, which individually do not challenge them. And, as achievement rises, some of our most prestigious universities report increasing difficulty in differentiating between very strong candidates for the most popular courses, since their educational records appear very similar.

2.17. Perhaps more seriously, there has been little choice of high-quality curriculum and qualifications pathways. The GCSE and A level route has been by far the most well-recognised and understood route to success. But for those who prefer to learn in a different way, who would benefit from greater variety of learning styles or who are more interested by learning in ways with direct practical applicability, there has not been real choice. These young people (although many might do well in GCSEs and A levels) have to wait to develop their talents until later in the education and training system.

2.18. For some pupils people in this category, achieving well in GCSEs and A levels enables them to flourish at university, on an academic or vocational course, and then to go on to success in employment. For others, though, the existing curriculum offer switches them off. They may take GCSEs without success. As Figure 2.6 shows, very few of those who do not get 5 or more A*-C GCSEs at 16 go on to study at level 3. Since the success rate for those retaking GCSEs is not high (only around 20% of those retaking get a higher grade than they did first time around), young people may easily get stuck in a qualifications blind alley. Furthermore, there is currently little scope to take a little more time over GCSEs in order to reach a higher standard.

2.19. The post-16 alternatives to GCSEs and A levels in schools and colleges need to be more widely available and to be credible with employers. Too many young people experience qualifications 'dead ends', where despite pursuing a further qualification, there

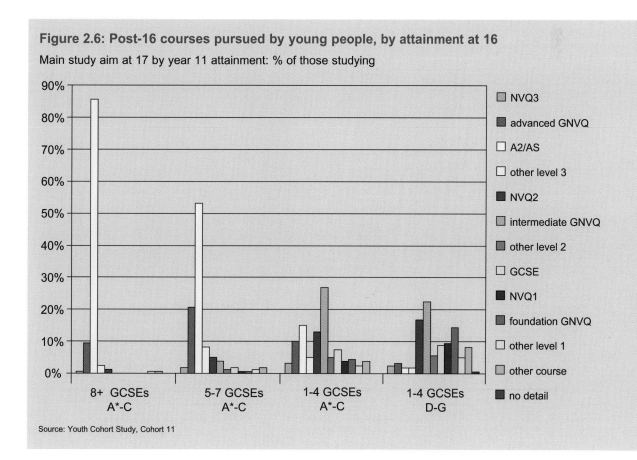

Figure 2.6: Post-16 courses pursued by young people, by attainment at 16

Main study aim at 17 by year 11 attainment: % of those studying

Legend: NVQ3, advanced GNVQ, A2/AS, other level 3, NVQ2, intermediate GNVQ, other level 2, GCSE, NVQ1, foundation GNVQ, other level 1, other course, no detail

Categories: 8+ GCSEs A*-C, 5-7 GCSEs A*-C, 1-4 GCSEs A*-C, 1-4 GCSEs D-G

Source: Youth Cohort Study, Cohort 11

are no clear onward routes to employment or progression to a higher level of learning.

Vocational education and training for young people have low credibility and status in this country

2.20. Vocational education has long been a cause of concern in this country. Ever since the implementation of the 1944 Education Act, when the proposed technical schools were not developed on the scale initially envisaged, successive policy initiatives have never been more than partially effective. Vocational education for young people has often failed to command the confidence of employers, higher education and the general public.

2.21. We have never had in this country a vocational education track that is as well understood as the academic one, nor one which has been seen as a naturally effective means of preparing young people for work or further study, even though it works well for some learners. That compares unfavourably with

many other advanced industrial countries, where the large numbers of young people pursuing vocational routes from the age of 14 onwards can have real confidence that what they are doing will be in demand from employers and from higher education establishments.

2.22. Successive policy initiatives over several decades have failed to resolve the issue. And although a number of awarding bodies offer qualifications that are respected, we are left with an alphabet soup of qualifications of different sizes, at different levels, with few clear progression routes between them. With the exception of Apprenticeships, nothing on offer in the vocational area has the clear appeal to young people, the public, employers and higher education (HE) of GCSEs and A levels. And, as Figure 2.7 shows, there is scope for considerable improvement in success rates for NVQ and apprenticeship provision.

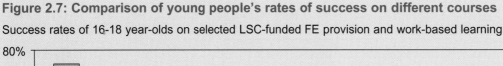

Figure 2.7: Comparison of young people's rates of success on different courses

Success rates of 16-18 year-olds on selected LSC-funded FE provision and work-based learning

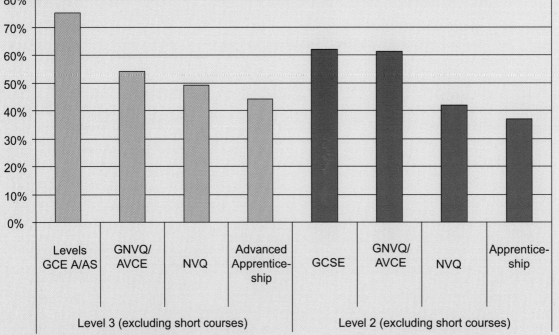

Source: DfES statistical first release further education and work-based learning for young people – learner outcomes in England: 2002/2003
Note: Apprenticeship success rates not directly comparable to the other qualifications.

Employers express concerns about basic skills

2.23. Employers have expressed real concerns about whether those who leave school at 16 with relatively few qualifications really have the basic skills, especially in maths and communication, which they will need for work. The evidence of the Skills for Life survey shows that among those with low or no qualifications in the adult population, literacy and numeracy levels are also low.

2.24. A range of strategies are in place to tackle the problem. Among adults, the Skills for Life strategy is having a real impact in improving literacy and numeracy. We exceeded our target for 750,000 learners to achieve a Skills for Life qualification.

2.25. The literacy and numeracy strategies in primary schools have transformed standards of achievement at age 11; and the Key Stage 3 National Strategy has been driving up achievement in the basics at age 14. Nonetheless, there is more to do if we are to ensure that no young person leaves school without a strong grounding in the basics they need for ordinary life and employment.

2.26. Those who progress further through the system, into A levels and higher education, are very much less criticised for lacking functional skills. Nonetheless, some universities are concerned that they do not have these skills at high enough levels – for example, they may be able to read and write well, but may be less strong at writing extended, analytical prose. It is sometimes argued that because the so-called 'compensatory' assessment system at GCSE means that a good grade can be achieved because strengths in one area compensate for weaknesses in another, GCSEs do not fully secure achievement in the functional core of maths and English.

There is concern about the assessment burden

2.27. Finally, some people argue that the overall amount of assessment in the system is now too great. At different times, the concern has been about the burden on students, the burden on teachers or the burden on the examination system of the volume of scripts. This was a particularly important issue following the introduction of the Curriculum 2000 A level reforms. The latest evaluation reports on Curriculum 2000, however, suggest that the system has bedded down and that students and teachers are generally more comfortable with the amount and type of assessment in most cases. And in the post-16 sector, our measures to reduce bureaucracy, led by Sir Andrew Foster, have sought to eradicate inappropriate assessment arrangements.

2.28. Taken together, therefore, despite the strengths of our education system and the progress that has been made, there are important issues to resolve.

Figure 2.8: Employer satisfaction[2] with the knowledge and skills of graduates and school leavers

	Graduates		School leavers	
	Satisfied	Dissatisfied	Satisfied	Dissatisfied[2]
Basic skills (low-level literacy and numeracy)	54%	8%	35%	23%
Key Skills (communication, team-working, problem solving, IT etc)	51%	8%	25%	24%
Self-management	34%	11%	10%	31%
Business awareness	26%	16%	6%	33%

Source: CBI employment trends survey (September 2002)

[2] Other responses available were 'neither satisfied nor dissatisfied' and 'not applicable'.

Chapter 3
Vision

Summary

We want all young people to be well prepared for later life through the education they receive. We want the education system to enable every young person to pursue their aspirations, and through hard work qualify themselves to succeed, equipping themselves with the skills and attributes that employers need.

In order to do this, we need to allow young people more choice, both of what to study and where to study. We want every young person to be motivated by a curriculum which allows them to learn in a style that suits them and to achieve qualifications as soon as they are ready, rather than at a fixed age. We want the qualifications that are available to carry real weight in the outside world – especially with employers and with higher education, so that they genuinely provide a ticket to later success.

This means that we need a system increasingly tailored to the needs of the individual pupil. Within that system, every young person must be supported to succeed in the basics – an essential grounding for life and work. Sixteen will cease to be a crucial point – as more young people accelerate; more take longer in order to achieve higher standards; and virtually all remain in learning to 18 and beyond. Young people should be able more readily to mix theoretical and practical styles of learning, but with confidence that the qualifications they achieve form a coherent package for further progression in education and into the workplace. As a key part of achieving this, we intend to improve vocational education and qualifications – offering interest and variety to many more young people and new routes to success.

We seek to ensure that all young people are stretched to achieve – whether by accelerating to higher levels of learning, increasing the breadth of their studies or by pursuing greater depth in the subjects they are learning – so that all are learning and doing their best. And we will increase our drive to re-engage those who are currently switched off by school.

3.1. We believe that every young person has potential; that the job of our education system is to develop and extend that potential; that in doing so, education must concern itself most of all about the future of young people and who they will become; that it must therefore enable young people to achieve and it must prepare them for life and for work, equipping them with the skills that employers need. We believe that there are many ways to achieve, and many ways to prepare young people for life and for work. We believe that all of these have dignity and value and deserve respect.

3.2. Our vision is therefore that our education system should provide every young person with a route to success in life through hard work and dedication.

3.3. To do so, it must provide opportunities that stretch and motivate each young person; interesting opportunities to learn in a variety of different ways – abstract and practical – and rigorous qualifications with currency in the worlds of work and of higher education, both here and abroad. A tailored 14-19 phase must mean that young people can pursue their aspirations, choose learning that is tailored to meet their needs and through study and hard work qualify themselves to achieve their aims.

3.4. At present the system does not provide that opportunity to all. By comparison with other countries, the English system does well by a proportion of young people who are engaged and motivated by conceptual study. It does much less well by those whose preferences are for learning which is more practical, with an obvious relevance and application to the wider world. The many young people for whom some opportunities to learn in this way would be beneficial, motivating or simply enjoyable have had no outlet for this preference. For some, the resulting curriculum causes them to switch off, even though they may do well at GCSE. For them, the curriculum and qualifications currently available do not provide a route to improving their life chances and they may drop out of further study at or shortly after the age of 16.

3.5. The burning challenge we face is to transform this picture, so that every young person is engaged by the learning opportunities they have, many more continue in education, and dropping out by the age of 17 becomes increasingly rare. We aim for a 14-19 system of education that allows our young people to exceed the standards achieved abroad, which allows them to make the most of their opportunities within a global society and a global economy, and to achieve high-quality, internationally-recognised qualifications.

We will strengthen 11-14 education

3.6. If we are to offer young people more choice at 14, we need to be confident that they are making that choice from the sound platform of a good general education. Our first priority is therefore to ensure that more of our 14 year-olds are well educated, by reforming the curriculum for 11-14 year-olds (**Key Stage 3**). More children are reaching the standards expected of them as 11 year olds – though it remains a priority to continue increasing that number – but too few of those who do not achieve that level catch up during Key Stage 3 (KS3). And too many young people do not find the early years of secondary school stretching and involving.

3.7. The compulsory curriculum is at its broadest in KS3. It is the moment when young people's understanding of the sciences should help them to make sense of the world around them; when they are introduced to some of the key writers in the English language, including Shakespeare; when they begin to develop a good sense of historical perspective and chronology, based on key facts and episodes in history; the ability to listen, speak, read and write to an acceptable standard in a modern foreign language; an understanding of the geography of the world around them.

3.8. We need more pupils to reach 14 with a good grounding in all of these. We also need to be sure that there is space in the timetable for those who need additional support to catch up in the basics. We need a KS3 curriculum which supports these goals.

There will be a wider choice of what and where to learn

3.9. Our next requirement for achieving this vision is that there should be much stronger **vocational** routes to success, which are genuinely valued by employers, and as providing access to higher education. This has been the historic weakness of our education system: not merely that vocational routes are seen by many young people as second class, but also that they are not seen by employers and universities as a sound preparation.

3.10. It does not have to be like this. In many other countries, vocational routes are well-trodden pathways into work and into higher education, where universities see vocational education as a strong basis for further study. And in this country too, many degree courses are vocational in nature – some of them, like law, medicine and engineering, among the most oversubscribed university courses available. Such degrees are well understood by young people, employers and the higher education world. We believe that vocational study before the age of 19 can achieve comparable acceptance and respect. It can prepare young people for a wide range of demanding and important careers in all sectors of the economy, from the technicians who are the lifeblood of laboratories and industry, to designers working in fashion and publishing.

3.11. We intend that young people will have real choice from the age of 14. Between 14 and 16, whatever choices they make, they should experience a broad curriculum which prepares them well for future life and learning. Whichever route they take, they will not narrow down their options – and will be able to make a further choice about how to continue in learning. By the age of 19, young people will have had the opportunity to pursue academic

qualifications; qualifications in a broad vocational area; or occupationally-specific qualifications in the work context. Whichever way they choose to become qualified, the qualifications they achieve will have real currency.

3.12. In opening up these wider opportunities, we will address the risks. We cannot have young people making such narrow choices at the age of 14 that they cannot later change tack. So all the pathways must remain broad, at least until the age of 16 – and must give young people transferable skills. We cannot have young people ignorant of what is available or unable to make choices that are good for them. We cannot return to the days before the National Curriculum when boys and girls sometimes had little opportunity to study in areas which had been the traditional preserve of the other sex. So good quality and impartial information, advice and guidance are crucial.

Education must ensure that all young people learn the English and maths they need for life

3.13. In this world of wider choice and broader opportunity for young people, we must ensure that every young person gets the preparation they need for later life, not just the opportunity to do what interests them. Above all, this means that we need every young person to achieve high standards in the **basics** of functional English and maths in particular. In the forthcoming Skills White Paper, we will set out how we will match this focus on functional skills for young people with a similar focus for adults who have been failed in the past.

3.14. Without these basics for modern life, no young person can consider themselves truly educated. Without these basics, no-one can make the most of everyday life or better themselves at work. Without these basics, no-one will be able to progress to learn as much as they otherwise could, whatever their other abilities. So, we intend to raise the bar, to ask more of schools, colleges and young people in this area – so that no-one thinks that a broad package of qualifications without these basics can suffice. No-one who is capable should leave education or training without achieving functional mastery of English and maths.

3.15. This focus on the basics does not represent a diminution of creativity or other skills: no novelist can become great without a strong command of English and no scientist or engineer can work without control of number. But education is not only about the basics. We are determined that the launch pad for the greater range of options of the new 14-19 phase should be that young people have a sound grounding by the age of 14 in all the National Curriculum subjects.

3.16. Throughout the 14-19 phase, it remains a priority that young people can pursue these subjects. In our increasingly scientific and technological world, we continue to put science at the heart of education – as a compulsory subject in the National Curriculum in Key Stage 4 and have made it a priority to encourage more young people to take it up post-16. And we already have in place statutory entitlements to study modern foreign languages, the humanities, the arts, and design and technology. We will make sure that all of these are available to all young people.

3.17. Beyond these subjects, we need to be confident that everyone leaving education is equipped to be an informed, responsible, active citizen. In an ever more complex, interdependent world, where an engaged population is crucial to the health of our society, we continue to put citizenship at its heart too. And we need real confidence that our schools and colleges really do give young people the skills they need for employability – for a young person who is not employable has few opportunities in life – and for further learning.

Qualifications will be achieved as soon as young people are ready – 16 will cease to be the crucial age

3.18. We must **stretch** every young person to achieve. This country is unusual internationally in that young people typically take a qualification at 16. But there are real benefits to that – there is no doubt that many young people work hard between the ages of 14 and 16 so that they succeed at GCSE. But while some young people are not sufficiently stretched (and so in some cases acquire very long lists of often similar GCSEs), others struggle to get there at all by 16.

3.19. So our vision is that 16 should cease to be a fixed point in our system at which all young people take qualifications – more and more should do so as soon as they are ready. That may mean a faster pace – doing some qualifications early and moving on to study at the next level, deepening or broadening their studies having achieved a qualification or a combination of these. It may mean taking a little longer in order to achieve higher standards.

3.20. Crucially, we want a system in which no young people get stuck in a qualifications blind alley. There are currently too many examples of qualifications from which there is no way for young people to progress – either to further study or into meaningful employment.

We will re-engage those who currently drop out

3.21. Our final key task is to tackle **disengagement**. Some 9% of young people aged 16-19 are not in education, employment or training. By providing a more motivating set of options of where and when to study, we will increase the desire of more young people to stay within the training system. By tackling the personal problems of young people through the 'Every Child Matters' programme, we will progressively lower the barriers to their achievement. And we will seek to make sure that we develop options for the most disengaged young people which gradually draw them back into learning, with support.

We will configure the system to deliver

3.22. If these are the aims at the heart of our vision, then we take seriously our responsibility to configure the system around these aims, so that we make new opportunities available to young people, wherever they might be. Our priorities are not focused on the current institutional arrangements, but on the breadth and quality of what is available to young people.

3.23. In practice, this will mean that area by area, institutions will need to come together to decide how to make an offer best meeting the talents and aspirations of young people. Together, they will make a better and broader offer to young people than they could do alone.

3.24. At the same time, we will ensure that every school and college is held to account for the quality of what it delivers and pushed to improve. There will be no relaxation of our determination to ensure that every educational establishment is a good one and we will broaden our expectations of schools and colleges to make use of other available courses and facilities if that is in the interests of young people.

3.25. The degree of change implied by this agenda is significant. It will be neither a simple nor a short-term task. A key measure of our success will be that we do not in any way damage public confidence in the education and exam system as we make the changes. It will be equally important that the teachers and others who will be crucial to making the changes work have the support that they need to do so and are not overloaded with change, so that they can continue to offer their best to the young people in their care.

Our principles

3.26. In the light of this vision, we can now set out our principles for this White Paper and for the programme of change that flows from it:

- We want to give all young people the opportunity to achieve success in life through hard work regardless of their gender, ethnicity or family circumstances. This means:

  - we want every young person to be secure in the basics that they will need for life and work;

  - we want all young people to enjoy their learning, to be stretched to achieve and to be rewarded for success;

  - all learning programmes should have clear progression routes to further learning. We want young people to leave learning with the skills that employers need;

  - we want young people to have a choice of where and what to learn, reflecting their own talents and aptitudes; and

  - we will make sure that the organisational arrangements follow the needs of learners and reflect their diversity.

- We value the current generation of young people as fully as future generations. This means:

  - we will implement our proposed changes as soon as is practicable, so that more young people have the opportunity to benefit from them;

  - but we will manage change carefully, so that the education system is not unnecessarily disrupted.

- We will ensure that the workforce can implement what they are asked to do. This means:

    - we will make sure that we continue to have a properly trained workforce, by offering training and support to existing and future teachers, lecturers and others in the workforce; and

    - we will manage the effect of these changes on the workforce, ensure that schools and colleges are able to deploy staff to match skills to needs, so that they are not overloaded.

3.27. These principles underpin the proposals in this White Paper. They are at the heart of our ambition for transforming opportunity for today's young people.

Chapter 4
A strong foundation at Key Stage 3

Summary

We want more young people to reach the age of 14 with a strong grounding in the basics and engaged by education. In order to achieve this, we will:

- review the Key Stage 3 (KS3) curriculum, to improve its coherence in subjects where there are problems, to reduce the overall level of prescription and allow more scope for schools to stretch their pupils and to help those who fall behind expected standards to catch up;

- through the Secondary National Strategy and the New Relationship with Schools, ensure that schools are supported and challenged to use this additional freedom wisely;

- strengthen our emphasis on English and maths, in particular by expecting schools to focus systematically on those pupils who arrive from primary school below the expected level;

- continue to publish results in KS3 tests in English, maths and science and introduce a new online test in ICT; and

- provide professional development for teachers to support their assessment of pupils in the other subjects; and produce a 'Pupil Profile' for pupils and parents, recording their achievement across the curriculum.

By doing so, we will ensure that more young people achieve National Curriculum level 5 in English, maths, science and ICT; and that all young people are stretched to achieve.

4.1. In the new 14-19 system, it will be increasingly important that young people have very strong foundations and a good general education by the age of 14. From then on, they will be making wider choices in an increasingly tailored system, which means that the groundwork must be laid in the early years of secondary education (ie at KS3). For young people to succeed later, their experiences up to the age of 14 must prepare them well and leave them with an enthusiasm for further learning. Most importantly, they need to begin the 14-19 phase with the skills and knowledge to make the most of the opportunities available. That must include a good grounding in all the foundation subjects of the National Curriculum.

4.2. So, the changes we propose 14-19 will demand changes 11-14 as well. Children enter secondary school with a range of different achievements and experiences. Getting everyone to the starting line of the 14-19 phase means that we need more tailoring of education before 14. So, we begin our proposals in this White Paper by setting out

what we want for our 14 year olds: what we think they will need in order to succeed later; and how we propose to make sure that many more of them have that sound foundation.

The educated 14 year-old

4.3. Our vision of educated 14 year olds is simply expressed. First and foremost, we want them to have achieved high standards in the basics, because without these, we know that young people do not flourish in education, employment or life. Second, we want them to have a broad range of knowledge across a rich curriculum. Third, we want to be confident that every young person has experienced a range of learning opportunities within and outside school. As a result, we want young people to be enthusiastic and expert learners and to continue learning and developing their skills throughout their adult lives.

High standards in the basics

4.4. Standards of achievement in English, maths, science and ICT at 14 have been steadily improving. From 1999 to 2004, the number of 14 year olds achieving National Curriculum level 5 rose by 7 percentage points in English, 11 points in maths and 11 in

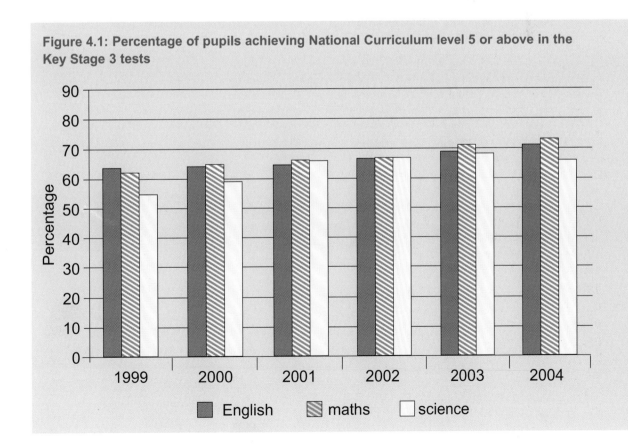

Figure 4.1: Percentage of pupils achieving National Curriculum level 5 or above in the Key Stage 3 tests

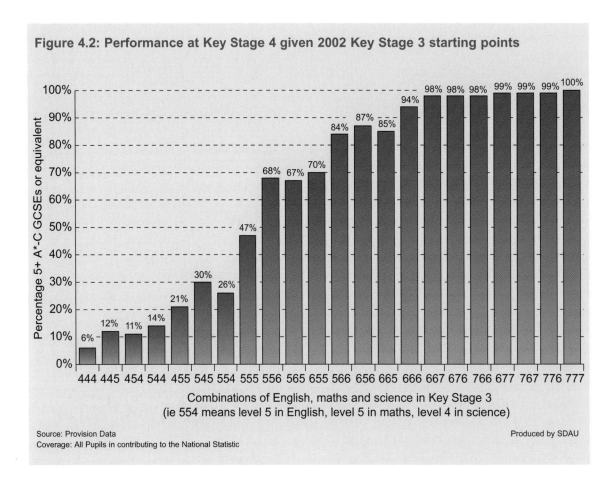

Figure 4.2: Performance at Key Stage 4 given 2002 Key Stage 3 starting points

Combinations of English, maths and science in Key Stage 3
(ie 554 means level 5 in English, level 5 in maths, level 4 in science)

Source: Provision Data
Coverage: All Pupils in contributing to the National Statistic

Produced by SDAU

science, as Figure 4.1 shows. It remains a priority to do more. We want everyone who can, to achieve at least level 5 at this age, since that is what is needed to make the most of upper secondary education. As Figure 4.2 shows, few young people who do not achieve

English and maths at National Curriculum level 5

This is a summary of the standards that learners at level 5 should demonstrate in English and maths. The full descriptions for all subjects are available on the National Curriculum website: www.nc.uk.net

English

Pupils talk and listen confidently in a wide range of contexts, including some that are of a formal nature. Pupils show understanding of a range of texts, identifying key features, themes, information and characters. Pupils' writing is varied and interesting, conveying meaning clearly in a range of forms for different readers, using a more formal style where appropriate.

Maths

In order to carry through tasks and solve mathematical problems, pupils identify and obtain necessary information. They check their results, considering whether these are sensible. Pupils can add, subtract, multiply and divide with decimals to two places and can calculate fractional or percentage parts of quantities. Pupils can multiply and divide any three-digit number by any two-digit number without a calculator. They know the rough metric equivalents of imperial units still in daily use. They make sensible estimates of a range of measures in relation to everyday situations.

level 5 at 14 go on to get 5 A*-C grade GCSEs. Our target is that 85% of 14 year olds should achieve level 5 or above in English, maths and ICT, and 80% in science by 2007; with at least 50% of pupils in all schools doing so by 2008.

4.5. The quality of teaching and learning has improved as a result of the Key Stage 3 National Strategy. In March 2004 Ofsted reported that, "the Strategy is helping to improve teaching… Teachers welcome the training and support the Strategy provides". In the light of this success we are extending the Strategy to become the Secondary National Strategy, providing support at Key Stage 4 too. Additional funding will ensure that this does not dilute our focus on KS3.

4.6. In addition to functional skills, young people need a range of learning and social skills. Success in further and higher education and in employment depends on the ability to adapt to new or changing circumstances. Independent learning skills are essential for study at university level. Businesses want skilled and enthusiastic employees who can help them respond to the rapidly changing demands of a competitive global economy. These skills are not separately taught, but brought out by expert teachers through the methods they use to teach the curriculum subjects.

A broad range of knowledge across a rich curriculum

4.7. The National Curriculum is at its broadest in KS3. The study of the sciences becomes more formalised and intensive – and pupils should begin to develop a scientific understanding of many aspects of the world around them. It is the moment at which they are introduced to some of the key writers in the English language, including Shakespeare. They develop skills of reading and writing, speaking and listening in a modern foreign language – and as our modern foreign languages strategy is implemented in full, they are increasingly doing so from a higher base. They develop historical understanding,

including a sense of chronology and of some of the most famous episodes of the past. They develop an understanding of the human and physical geography of the world. They learn to compose, perform and appreciate music. They develop the skills to produce and manipulate products in a variety of materials. They study art and produce their own works in a variety of styles and forms.

4.8. We are committed to this breadth of study and want every pupil to have a high-quality learning experience in all these subjects. We will continue our work to improve teaching and learning in them, building on the successes of the Key Stage 3 National Strategy. Links to activities outside school are important too. The Music Manifesto set out our commitment to improve access to music through a range of experiences within and beyond the curriculum. Our PE and School Sport Strategy will give children two hours of sport each week and better access to local sports clubs.

4.9. All of the foundation subjects of the National Curriculum provide knowledge and understanding which are an essential preparation for further study and for adult life. As we introduce greater flexibility into the curriculum after the age of 14, it becomes all the more important that young people have been well taught in these subjects by the time they are 14. Our objective is that in future, they have a better understanding of these subjects and their key concepts than they do now.

4.10. The compulsory elements of the curriculum also provide the foundations of citizenship. Through study of citizenship, young people develop as informed and responsible citizens with the knowledge, skills and attitudes to play an effective role in society. Through personal, social and health education (PSHE), they develop the knowledge, skills and understanding they need to lead healthy, confident and independent lives. Religious education encourages pupils to develop their sense of indentity and belonging, to develop respect and sensitivity to others, enabling them to flourish individually and as citizens within their communities.

The London Student Pledge

The London Student Pledge aims to widen the experiences and aspirations of all young people in the capital. The local authority and schools in each borough are working with local organisations to provide opportunities to learn across 10 broad areas of activity, inside and outside school. These are:

- contributing views on London issues;
- recognition of students' early success;
- taking part in a display seen by an audience (sports, music, dance or visual arts);
- experience involving the spoken word;
- residential experience;
- experience of volunteering;
- experience of attending an arts or sports event as part of the audience;
- experience of other languages and cultures;
- experience of seeing a practical project through from beginning to end; and
- experience of cutting-edge science and technology.

4.11. We continue to stress the importance of all the subjects at this stage and want to ensure that everyone is engaged and stretched by the subject teaching they receive. Achieving at National Curriculum level 5 across the curriculum is the preparation everyone needs; being supported to achieve more where they can is the key for motivating them.

A range of learning opportunities

4.12. Learning at school should be enriched by a range of activities beyond the curriculum.

The London Student Pledge provides an example of the sort of enrichment activities that many areas provide. We are developing proposals to build on the extensive range of study support, clubs and other activities that schools already offer, supporting schools and other organisations like libraries and museums, to broaden the range of activities and facilities available. We will set out our proposals for doing so in due course.

Raising attainment in English, maths and science at Chestnut Grove

Chestnut Grove is an 11-19 mixed comprehensive visual arts college based in Balham, South London. The focus of its two-year KS3 is on raising attainment in English, maths and science.

In English, students are taught the key objectives in years 7 and 8. All students then sit an exam in year 8. In 2004, 100% of year 8 pupils achieved at least level 5 in English and 39% achieved a level 6 or better. Now in year 9, the pupils have used the curriculum space created to take part in the "Shakespeare in Schools Festival", where they performed Othello, and they are studying utopian novels.

In maths, the college has taken a different approach. Those students who enter at level 3 or below receive focused support in year 7 to ensure that they have grasped the basic concepts which make up the level 4 objectives. Pupils who have already achieved a level 4 or above cover a curriculum consisting of the level 5 and 6 objectives. "The lessons in maths are good fun, we always do new things", says Luke, year 7.

Improving the geography curriculum

Ofsted's 2002/03 geography report identified several weaknesses in KS3 including an over-emphasis on the coverage of content, which was not always coherent. This could limit opportunities to develop independent learning skills and to stretch pupils. We will ask the QCA to advise us on how to address these weaknesses. The options include:

- more focus on key geographical concepts to bring greater meaning to subject content and engage and excite students;

- a reduction in overlapping objectives and prescribed examples, allowing space to explore current real world issues in depth; and

- more choice for teachers over some parts of the content, so they can better tailor lessons to their pupils' needs, interests and aptitudes.

Following QCA's advice we will work with subject experts and leading teachers to develop better guidance and training for geography teachers. We want to help them to teach the curriculum in a way that engages and excites pupils, increasing progression by developing their skills and understanding.

A new Key Stage 3

4.13. Significant improvements have been made to the quality of teaching at KS3 in recent years through the National Strategy, and more 14 year-olds than ever before achieve the standards we aspire to. But the design of the curriculum has some significant problems. Some programmes of study are less coherent than they could be and some material is repeated in different subjects. The amount of prescription leaves schools with little space to timetable catch-up provision for those who are struggling, and to offer really stretching opportunities for those who have particular gifts and talents. Some young people who enter secondary school below the expected standard fall further behind, because they lack the skills and knowledge necessary to access parts of the KS3 curriculum. It is a crucial priority that schools should provide focused support, so that these young people catch up as quickly as possible.

4.14. We are therefore asking QCA to undertake a review of the KS3 curriculum. We are clear that all of the existing foundation subjects will remain in the curriculum and that we want more pupils to be well educated in all of them. However, the review must create more space in the timetable to ensure that the curriculum: enables those who had fallen behind at 11 to catch up in the basics; allows

everyone to be stretched; and increases the number who have a good understanding of all the subjects in the curriculum.

4.15. We need more young people to be interested in studying science. At present, the curriculum sets out a long shopping list of facts to be learnt. Not only the key conceptual underpinnings of the subject, but also its excitement, relevance and crucial importance are too easily lost. Just as we have worked with the science community to create a Key Stage 4 curriculum which will encourage more young people to continue to study the sciences, so we intend to do the same at KS3. We do not expect a reduction in the amount of time young people spend studying science at KS3.

4.16. Similar arguments can be made about the existing curriculum in subjects such as history and geography. In other subjects, including design and technology, there are heavy requirements on pupils to complete a large number of tightly specified tasks. A more coherent curriculum, with less duplication between subjects, will give teachers greater flexibility to focus more on progression throughout KS3 and raise aspirations.

4.17. This could mean quite significant changes in some subjects. But if we are to achieve our aims of more young people succeeding as they leave education, we believe that they are necessary. They build on the success of the Key Stage 3 National Strategy, which has improved progression and led to significant improvements in standards. They are the essential next step in ensuring that those who are behind in the basics at 11 catch up by 14.

4.18. We have already been piloting a range of different models. In particular, two pilots exploring curriculum innovations point the way to further improvements in teaching and learning. One is a pilot of injecting greater pace into the curriculum through a two-year KS3, where evidence from Ofsted shows that condensing the curriculum encourages better curriculum planning, reduces duplication in different subjects and releases time to broaden and enrich the curriculum in different ways to suit pupils with different abilities and learning styles. The other is a planned low-attainers pilot, designed to accelerate catch-up in schools where the children joining in year 7 had relatively low achievement in primary school.

4.19. Through the existing pilots we are developing a strong evidence base from which to work. We will build on this experience and extend our plans for pilots to test changes to KS3 that are in line with the aims of the QCA review, to ensure that it is informed by practical experience from schools. We will continue to use pilots as QCA undertake the review to ensure that its aims will be met in practice.

4.20. We will then make sure that all schools take advantage of the new flexibilities. We will do so by:

- supporting schools through the National Strategy, so that teachers have the materials they need and the professional development to help them deliver the new curriculum effectively;

- incentivising schools to get more young people to level 5 by 14, through the New Relationship with Schools, through continued publication of performance tables, including value-added information and through the Key Stage 3 targets; and

- incentivising stretch for the most able, both through the New Relationship with Schools and the measures it will introduce to hold schools more fully to account for stretching all young people, and through the work of the National Academy for Gifted and Talented Youth helping schools to meet the teaching challenges of gifted pupils.

4.21. Young people should also develop their personal and learning skills during KS3. These skills are not separately taught, but brought out through teaching the National Curriculum subjects – and the best teachers find ways to do so in every lesson. We will use the National Strategy's Leading in Learning programme to spread this best practice and develop a range of models to show how teachers in different subjects can help pupils develop these skills.

4.22. These skills will help young people to choose options at 14 suited to their interests and aptitudes, which will lead on to further learning and employment. We also set out in the next chapter our proposals to improve advice and guidance.

Assessment arrangements which support this

4.23. Most young people should be able to reach level 5 or above across the range of National Curriculum subjects by age 14. Achieving that goal should be a significant moment in their educational career. It will demonstrate that they have achieved the basic level of knowledge needed for further learning and to begin to become an effective citizen.

4.24. To emphasise the importance of a pupil's achievements by age 14, we want them to be recorded in summary form for pupils and parents in a simple Pupil Profile, including their achievement in every subject.

- For young people and their parents, the Pupil Profile will be a record of what they have achieved. It will highlight their strengths and show them any areas where they need to focus their efforts.

- For the institutions teaching young people from age 14, the Pupil Profile will show that they have learnt the foundations necessary to progress, or highlight any areas where they will need extra help to catch up.

4.25. Assessment at age 14 will be the underpinning of the 14-19 phase. It will show young people and their teachers how well prepared they are for the 14-19 phase of learning. In particular, it will be a trigger which ensures that young people who do not achieve level 5 in the basics devote time in their studies post-14 to get to that level as soon as possible and to go on to GCSE level.

4.26. Assessment at the end of KS3 is also a useful tool for teachers, lecturers and trainers. Increasing numbers of young people will be studying in more than one institution from age 14, including perhaps another nearby school, an FE college, or a work-based training provider. The performance data will help teachers to tailor their teaching to young people's needs.

Assessment in the core

4.27. A good level of knowledge and skill in English, maths, ICT and science are the most essential preparation for the 14-19 phase. Young people are formally assessed in English, maths and science at age 14. We are committed to maintaining external tests in these core subjects because they provide the most reliable and consistent measure available of what young people have achieved. We are also developing a test in ICT to build on the existing practice of teacher assessment. This will be an online assessment and will be electronically marked. It will be introduced alongside the other external tests at age 14 from 2008, subject to a successful pilot. Banks of optional teacher assessment tasks to enable the most able students to access the highest levels in the core subjects are already available and will be developed further.

4.28. We already publish schools' results in the English, maths and science tests in the Achievement and Attainment Tables.

Continuing to do so will be a strong incentive for schools to ensure that more young people reach expected standards. We will also publish results in the ICT test.

Assessment in the foundation subjects

4.29. Achievement in the foundation subjects is also important to provide the broad range of knowledge necessary for further study in the 14-19 phase. Teachers already assess young people throughout KS3 to ensure that they are progressing in the foundation subjects, to inform their teaching methods and to check whether they are reaching the expected standard at age 14.

4.30. We want to build on that practice and help teachers to improve their skills of assessment. Teachers make judgements about pupils' performance based on individual pieces of class work, longer projects and internally-set exams. However, the latest annual report of Her Majesty's Chief Inspector of Schools found that, "the use of assessment in meeting individual pupils' needs remains a weakness generally and is unsatisfactory in over a tenth of schools." We will examine models for supporting the professionalism of teachers in assessing students and for moderating teacher assessment at KS3, such as Chartered Examiners. We will provide training and guidance for teaching staff to develop their assessment skills and provide them with materials to help them accurately to assess student performance at all ability levels. This will include a bank of nationally developed standardised tests and activities, which we will ask QCA to produce, to support teachers' professional judgement in both summative and formative assessment.

4.31. Through these changes at KS3, we believe that more young people will reach the age of 14 with a sound grounding in the basics and a good understanding of the key concepts across the curriculum. More will receive a more personalised experience, and so will be more engaged with learning and better prepared for further study.

Chapter 5
A strong core 14-19

Summary

At the heart of 14-19 education will be an even sharper focus on the basics. Achieving level 2 (GCSE level) in English and maths is an essential part of a good education. In order to ensure more young people achieve that level:

- we have already reduced the level of prescription in the Key Stage 4 (KS4) curriculum, providing more scope for schools to support catch-up;

- we are extending the Key Stage 3 Strategy, so that it provides teaching materials and professional development across the secondary age range;

- we will introduce a general (GCSE) Diploma, awarded when young people achieve 5 A*-C grade GCSEs including English and maths (see Chapter 6);

- we will toughen the Achievement and Attainment Tables, showing what percentage of pupils have achieved the Diploma standard – ie 5 A*-C grade GCSEs *including* English and maths. We expect to phase out the existing 5 A*-C measure by 2008;

- we will ensure that no-one can get a C or better in English and maths without mastering the functional elements. Where a young person achieves the functional element only, we will recognise that separately;

- we will make sure that this functional core is the same in the adult Skills for Life qualifications, other Key Skills qualifications and in GCSEs; and

- we will provide more opportunities and incentives for young people who have not achieved level 2 by 16 to do so post-16 and support them in achieving level 1 or entry level qualifications as steps on the way.

5.1. There are some basic skills, knowledge and understanding that everyone needs in order to progress and succeed in learning, employment and life. First among these are a sound grounding in functional English and maths; but ICT skills, an understanding of the sciences and the knowledge and skills needed for citizenship, employment and further learning are also crucial. Together, these will remain compulsory for 14-16 year-olds.

5.2. We are renewing our focus on English and maths and particularly on the ability to apply them in everyday contexts. We want young people to reach at least GCSE level in English and maths and will challenge and support schools and colleges to deliver. In maths, we continue to be committed to the implementation of the Smith report and will continue to make it a priority that more young people progress on to advanced level and beyond.

5.3. We are also committed to improving GCSE science results and to increasing the number of young people taking science at advanced level and progressing to study science at university. It also remains a priority that all young people have a good grasp of science, so that they can make sense of the technological world we live in. Every young person will have a statutory entitlement to science study leading to two GCSEs and we expect that, as now, at least 80% of students will continue to take at least two science GCSEs, with many progressing to science courses at higher levels. We will take further action, if necessary to maintain the numbers of young people taking two science GCSEs.

5.4. Young people should have good opportunities to study a range of academic subjects. There are existing entitlements to study a modern foreign language; a humanities subject; design and technology; and the arts, as well as the complusory subjects. We re-confirm all of these as important to the 14-19 phase. We will also ensure that young people develop knowledge and skills to take their place in society. We will ensure that they are given opportunities to do so, both through more focused teaching of relevant curriculum subjects including citizenship and providing clearer guidance on the development of personal, and thinking and learning skills throughout the curriculum.

Functional English and maths

5.5. Functional English and maths are the English and maths that people need to participate effectively in everyday life, including in the workplace. Achieving National Curriculum level 5 in these skills by 14 is an important staging post, but people are only fully functional in English and maths when they have achieved the equivalent of a GCSE at grade C or higher (level 2 of the National Qualifications Framework). At level 2 they are able to apply their skills confidently in a range of different contexts.

5.6. We intend to ensure that schools focus on achievement in the basics. In Chapter 6, we set out our plans for a general (GCSE) Diploma, awarded when young people achieve 5 A*-C GCSEs including English and maths. We will toughen the performance tables to include an additional measure: the proportion of young people reaching this standard. We will pilot this change in 2005, with a view to full inclusion in the tables in 2006, alongside the existing 5 A*-C GCSEs (or equivalent). We expect to phase out the existing 5 A*-C measure by 2008.

5.7. We intend to ensure that young people receive support to reach this standard, especially where they haven't reached the expected level at 14. We will help schools to deliver this focused support by prioritising English and maths as we implement the Secondary National Strategy. This will support schools in curriculum organisation; will provide training and support to teachers; and will support whole school approaches, including the use of study support. Once established, the National Centre for Excellence in Mathematics Teaching will provide further support.

5.8. We will ensure that a grade C or better at GCSE is a guarantee that young people have the functional skills they need. We set out in

A whole-school approach to literacy and learning at Haybridge High School and Sixth Form

Haybridge High is an 11-18 mixed comprehensive in Worcestershire, which has adopted a whole-school approach to improving the literacy skills of all year groups, building on the principles of the Key Stage 3 National Strategy.

Strategy materials supported the work of each department in considering how to structure lessons and in adapting schemes of work to raise the profile of literacy skills. This included all classrooms displaying key words and all teachers using literacy-based activities at the start of lessons, insisting on corrections and correct vocabulary in the content of the subject.

Students have improved proficiency and confidence in reading, writing and interpretation, reflected in the 2004 results:

- 94% of students achieved 5+ A*-C grades at GCSE with 72% of them achieving 5+ A*-C grades including English and maths; and

- the school achieved an exceptional Key Stage 2 to GCSE value-added measure of 1042.1, placing Haybridge in the top 25% of schools nationally.

Chapter 7 our proposals for changes to GCSE to secure this. The redesigned qualifications will be available for first teaching in 2008 for English and 2009 for maths. Changes to maths will take place in the context of the implementation of Professor Adrian Smith's report 'Making Mathematics Count'.

5.9. We will ensure that young people can gain a qualification for achieving the functional skills, even if they are not able to achieve a full GCSE. QCA should secure the development of alternative qualifications, such as Skills for Life qualifications, to be studied alongside the KS4 programmes of study. We expect,

Examples from level 2 standards for adult literacy

Writing

- Present information and ideas in a logical or persuasive sequence, using paragraphs where appropriate.

- Use formal and informal language appropriate to purpose and audience.

- Use different styles of writing for different purposes, eg persuasive techniques, supporting evidence, technical vocabulary.

- Use correct grammar, eg subject-verb agreement, correct and consistent use of tense.

- Punctuate sentences correctly and use punctuation accurately, eg commas, apostrophes, inverted commas in a wide range of documents.

Examples from level 2 standards for adult numeracy

Understanding and using mathematical information

- Use numbers, fractions, decimal and percentages in the context of measures, estimating amounts and proportions, and make accurate observations.

- Use shape and space to record relevant measurements and make accurate observations.

- Use discrete and continuous data from tables, charts, diagrams and line graphs.

- Select and use appropriate mathematical tests, skills or concepts.

however, that most students should continue to complete a full GCSE.

5.10. We will work with employers and universities, as well as teachers and lecturers and subject specialists to describe clearly what is to be understood as functional skill and make sure that this definition is applied in all qualifications, covering all ages. The KS4 curriculum, the Key Skills qualifications and the Skills for Life standards and qualifications provide a good starting point. The examples on the previous page from the level 2 standards for adult literacy and numeracy set out the kinds of things we would expect functional English and maths to cover.

5.11. Post-16 learners already have an entitlement to study literacy and numeracy. We expect schools and colleges to provide continuing support to students to help them reach at least level 2 functional English and maths.

ICT skills

5.12. In addition to functional English and maths, the modern world and economy requires all young people to be competent in the use of ICT. ICT is part of the KS4 National Curriculum and has a statutory programme of study, reflected in GCSE ICT being taken by increasing numbers of students. GCSE ICT should be reviewed in a similar way to English and maths to identify a functional skills unit, building on the ICT Key Skills qualification and the ICT Skills for Life standards. For those not taking GCSE ICT, the functional unit should be available as a qualification in its own right and the KS4 programme of study should be reviewed to support this. Students should develop ICT skills across the curriculum.

Science

5.13. The 'Ten Year Science and Innovation Investment Framework' set out the Government's strategy for sustaining a strong supply of scientists and engineers. We are committed to contributing to that strategy by improving the quality of science teachers and lecturers in every school, college and

university, improving the results of students studying science at GCSE level and increasing the number of people choosing to study science, engineering and technology subjects in post-16 and higher education.

5.14. Science will remain compulsory at KS4 and it remains our firm expectation that at least 80% of students should do at least two science GCSEs. Indeed, to secure that, we will introduce a new statutory entitlement for all students to study science programmes leading to at least two GCSEs.

5.15. We have worked with the science community to develop a new programme of study for science at KS4 to be taught in schools from September 2006. The revised programme of study has a core which focuses on scientific literacy and provides options for further study and for links with other subject areas. A new suite of GCSEs based on the KS4 programme of study has been developed, as set out in Chapter 7.

5.16. These curriculum changes will be supported in schools through the Secondary National Strategy. Specialist Schools also have a key role to play in improving students' experience of science. Science, engineering, technology and mathematics and computing Specialist Schools already place an additional emphasis on science and we expect them to provide support to raise the quality of science in other schools within their areas.

5.17. These measures are intended to raise attainment at 16 and increase the number of students going on to study science post-16. We will keep under review their success in doing so and if necessary take further steps to boost participation and attainment in science post-16. In addition, we will seek to address the particular problem of poor uptake of physics among girls. Working in partnership with the Department of Trade and Industry and the Institute of Physics, we will commission research into why girls do not do physics, what can be done in the classroom to change this and the role that Science Learning Centres will play.

Bringing science to life at Treviglas Community College and Newquay Zoo

Treviglas Community College is an 11-18 mixed comprehensive in Newquay. Many of its students remain living and working in the area after completing their studies. The college wanted to engage its students, raise attainment and forge links with the local economy using GCSEs in vocational subjects, including applied science.

An early business partner was Newquay Zoo. Breeding records of their collection of 20 Humboldt penguins were used to help students learn about genetics. Working together, the school and zoo matched relevant parts of the course specification to the penguins and produced a workbook that students could take with them on their on-site visits.

Visiting the zoo brought the science to life. Students learned about the penguins and explored the zoo looking for other examples of selective breeding. In 2004, 52% of students got 5 GCSEs at A*-C, 6% more than had been expected to do so based on their previous performance. 32 of the 33 students who took applied science passed, with 52% getting A*-C.

5.18. Beyond the age of 16, we are taking action through the Success for All strategy to improve teaching in key curriculum areas such as science to ensure the best possible learning experience for young people.

Preparation for society

5.19. We want young people to be well equipped to participate in society and the wider world. The KS4 requirements in RE, PE, sex education, citizenship and the non-statutory framework for personal, social and health education (PSHE) provide a foundation of knowledge and skills crucial to living, learning and working in modern society. Education about sustainable development, for example, can help young people to understand the consequences of their actions for themselves and others, both in their own communities and globally.

5.20. We also recognise the importance of personal finance education in enabling young people to develop the financial capability they need to make informed judgements and to take effective decisions regarding the use and management of money in adult and working life. A range of subjects such as maths, PSHE, citizenship, business studies and careers education all offer good opportunities and contexts for exploring and improving young people's understanding of financial issues. The new Enterprise Education initiative further underscores the importance of financial capability as a context for, and key underpinning of, enterprise capability, along with economic and business understanding. And in line with the emphasis on improving functional skills, the Department has asked the QCA, as part of the wider review of GCSE maths, to consider including financial capability more explicitly in the maths curriculum. The new National Centre for Excellence in the Teaching of Mathematics, which is under development, will provide an important focus for supporting effective teaching of maths in schools and colleges, including functional maths, and we will ask the Centre to develop better support for personal financial education in the maths curriculum. Through these steps, we will support the work being undertaken by the 'Schools Project' which is part of the UK 'Strategy for Financial Capability' being co-ordinated by the Financial Services Authority.

5.21. There are clear links between RE, PE, sex education, citizenship and PSHE, and learners benefit when the links are emphasised in the way in which they are taught. Teaching the subjects in a co-ordinated way can also help to free up time within the curriculum. In 'Opportunity and Excellence' we said that we would support schools in taking a more joined-up approach to these subjects and in 2004 the QCA published guidance. We will ask QCA to review the impact of this guidance and to consider what further guidance or support is necessary.

Thinking and learning skills

- Enquiry, includes: asking relevant questions, planning and testing conclusions.

- Creative thinking, includes: suggesting hypotheses, imaginatively challenging ideas.

- Information processing, includes: locating and classifying information.

- Reasoning, includes: explaining opinions, actions and decisions, using deduction.

- Evaluation, includes: assessing evidence, judging against criteria and values.

Personal skills

- Communication and personal presentation for a range of audiences.

- Diligence, reliability and capability to improve, includes: organisation, initiative and willingness to learn.

- Working with others, includes: negotiating, awareness of others' needs, leadership.

- Moral and ethical awareness, includes: understanding right and wrong, responsibilities to family and community and their own potential.

5.22. Young people also need to develop their personal skills and a set of thinking and learning skills. Personal skills are those which give young people the ability to manage themselves and to develop effective social and working relationships. Thinking and learning skills mean knowing how to learn independently and adapt to a range of circumstances. Together these skills are essential for raising standards, further learning, employment and dealing with a range of real-world problems. We have worked with QCA to develop an outline description of these skills, building on the notion of Common Knowledge Skills and Attributes (CKSA) developed by the Working Group on 14-19 Reform, and on existing National Curriculum guidance.

5.23. These skills and attitudes are not confined to particular subjects, but can be developed throughout the curriculum at all ages. They are fundamental to improving young people's employability as well as their learning. Many teachers and lecturers are able to develop young people's thinking and learning skills and personal skills as part of the teaching and learning process. Taking part in wider activities beyond the curriculum can also foster these skills. However, Ofsted and QCA have raised concerns that they are not

consistently developed throughout all schools, colleges and work-based learning providers or at all ages.

5.24. We believe that the development of these skills is particularly important to delivering the five outcomes we have said we want for all young people as part of 'Every Child Matters' (see Figure 5.1). We believe that a more systematic approach to these skills will help, and will ask QCA to work with employers to develop them further into a single framework of skills covering all abilities. We will help teachers and lecturers to develop effective ways to teach and assess these skills building on the support for pedagogy already available through the National Strategies and Success for All.

5.25. We made work-related learning a statutory requirement in the curriculum from September 2004, and are investing an extra £180 million in enterprise education from September 2005, because we are determined that pupils of all abilities and talents will develop their employability skills and attitudes and their enterprise capability, and do so with employer input to their learning and in the environment of work. We want close ties between pupils' experience of work-related

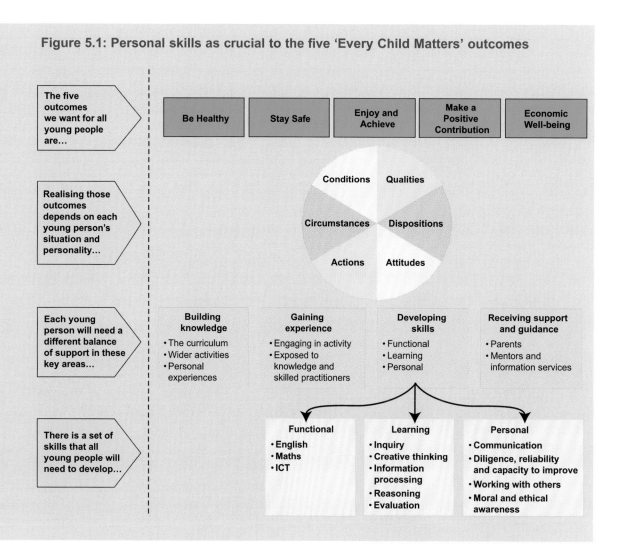

Figure 5.1: Personal skills as crucial to the five 'Every Child Matters' outcomes

learning and their careers advice and guidance. During 2005 we will consult all stakeholders on proposals for reform to engage more employers more effectively in young people's learning.

Information, advice and guidance

5.26. The Working Group said that it was crucial for young people to have high-quality and impartial information and guidance to get the most out of their learning, to enable successful progression from one stage to another and to inform the important choices that young people make between different options. We agree. We are setting out a clear route to improving choice for young people and their parents – in terms of both what and where to study. If young people are to get the most out of that choice, then we must be sure that:

- every young person understands the options open to them and their potential implications;

- the direct influences on young people, including parents, teachers and the peer group, support them to make decisions which work well for them in the long term; and

- young people develop the knowledge, skills and attitudes they need to make good choices, determined by their aptitudes and the needs of employers, rather than stereotypes about their gender or background.

5.27. To meet these objectives we will need:

- **Better basic information about options.** We are setting out in this White Paper plans for a national entitlement. This, together with our plans to rationalise qualifications should make the provision of basic information easier. We set out in Chapter 11 plans to develop a website setting out the choices, linked through in each area to an online local prospectus, which will set out the detail of how to access the offer.

- **Better information from employers about career routes.** A key element in our plans will be a leading role for employers in defining what they see as important for progression to particular careers. This will help young people understand better what they need to achieve if they are to get the kind of job they want.

- **A better-integrated curriculum.** In this chapter, we have set out our aims of making sure that schools bring out the connections between citizenship, work-related learning, careers education and PSHE as they are taught. We also want to be sure that young people have some direct experiences of the workplace which they can draw on when making choices about employment and learning.

- **Early intervention.** Young people begin tacitly to make choices early – not irrevocably, but removing certain options from the equation by an early stage, so that the boundaries within which later choices are made have been narrowed. Young people starting year 11 with the view that they will leave education very rarely change their mind over that year. Similarly, we might expect young people's decisions about learning from 14 to be formed by year 9. So, information and guidance will be in place from the start of secondary school.

5.28. To deliver these requirements we will need to support parents so that they also have the information and understanding to support their children. We should also exploit the power of the peer group, for example by training peer tutors in KS4 to work with young people in KS3 about what is available and what the implications of different choices are. We need to improve advice from home institutions and intend to introduce a professional development programme for teachers which boosts their ability to advise and which gives them good information about choices in their area. And we need to secure objectivity and impartiality in the advice young people receive, through providing other sources of advice.

5.29. We also need to help young people assess themselves and improve their decision-making abilities. Models which use coaching and mentoring rather than simple advice-giving have also shown their potential. And we need to disseminate good practice throughout the system – Ofsted has recently said that good advice and support of young people is a particular strength of further education colleges, and some schools in 14-19 pathfinder areas have developed excellent advice and guidance.

5.30. In the forthcoming Skills White Paper, we will set out developments which will aim to improve information for adults and so provide a better joined up service from youth to adulthood. We will set out our plans for delivering these proposals in due course.

Chapter 6
Routes to success for all

Summary

Our intention is to create an education system tailored to the needs of the individual pupil, in which young people are stretched to achieve, are more able to take qualifications as soon as they are ready, rather than at fixed times, and are more able to mix academic, practical and work-based styles of learning.

We will:

- introduce greater choice of what and where to study and make it easier to combine academic and vocational learning;

- retain GCSEs and A levels as cornerstones of the new system;

- introduce new specialised Diplomas, including vocational material and GCSEs and A levels where appropriate and covering each occupational sector of the economy. The Diplomas will be available at levels 1 (foundation), 2 (GCSE) and 3 (advanced);

- put employers and HE in the lead in designing specialised Diplomas through Sector Skills Councils which provide the right grounding for work and further study, supported by QCA;

- raise the bar by introducing a general (GCSE) Diploma, which will require achievement of 5 A*-C grade GCSEs, or equivalent, including English and maths; and

- challenge and support schools to ensure that young people take qualifications when they are ready, ending 16 as a fixed point in the system, encouraging acceleration and ensuring early achievement is recognised in Achievement and Attainment Tables and elsewhere.

6.1. Our aim is an engaging education system, more tailored to the talents and aptitudes of young people. We want more young people to be motivated by learning; more to be pursuing courses that interest them; and all of them to be pursuing qualifications that will stand them in good stead for later life. We already know, from the work that has been taking place between many schools and colleges over recent years, that offering young people more choice of what and where to learn, and making available opportunities to learn in a range of different ways – theoretical and practical – can be motivating for many young people.

6.2. We know that there is great variation in the achievement of young people by class, gender and ethnicity. We believe that our focus on the needs of the individual pupil will serve all young people well. It will be of particular value to groups of young people who currently achieve less well.

It will be easier to mix academic and vocational learning

6.3. The idea that there is, or should be, a clear dividing line between the academic and the vocational does not stand up to scrutiny. In HE, this has been obvious for some time. Many of the highest status and most demanding degree courses are vocational, but with significant academic content. Law, medicine and engineering are perhaps the most obvious examples among the traditional degree courses, but there are many others.

6.4. Nonetheless, there are still, of course, significant differences between the most theoretical and the most practical forms of education and training. For young people, practical learning offers them additional chances to succeed in education and prepare themselves for life. More practical, work-related learning motivates a large group of learners to achieve and progress. An engineering course focused on teaching young people how to use high-tech equipment, taught by a professional engineer in a workplace, is likely to be a very attractive experience for many. It is one that can engage young people who would otherwise switch off; offer those who enjoy practical work a chance to pursue their interests; and add variety, interest and value to a mainly academic programme.

6.5. We therefore need to continue to increase the range of options we offer young people about what and where to learn. Over the last few years, mixing academic and vocational learning at school has become increasingly common. Through the Increased Flexibility Programme, in 14-19 pathfinder areas and in other ways, schools and colleges have increasingly worked together to offer young people more choice of curriculum and qualifications. The introduction of new GCSEs in vocational subjects strengthens further the range of options and styles of learning available.

6.6. However, establishing routes which are really tailored to young people depends on a transformation of opportunity in vocational education – the most important task facing us in 14-19 education. We need to make it a real choice for all young people to pursue vocational courses, not something which is seen as a second-class route for those who cannot succeed on academic courses. We want to create a very high quality route, which mixes academic and vocational study as appropriate, leading to qualifications valued by employers and universities and therefore an attractive choice for young people. This will be the key to preparing more young people to succeed in life and to make a productive contribution to society.

All qualifications available to young people will have value as routes into higher education and employment

6.7. In order to support the more flexible phase we envisage, we need a range of qualifications which reward different types of learning, offering all young people stretching options. GCSEs and A levels are internationally respected. They will be kept as a cornerstone of 14-19 learning. They will continue to be assessed through rigorous external examinations; and they will be reformed to increase stretch and challenge and to improve progression.

6.8. However, the more tailored 14-19 phase we envisage does require significant change in other qualifications. We want all young people to be pursuing programmes leading to qualifications which enable them to progress further in learning and which are in demand from employers and universities. It is too difficult at present for young people to put together for themselves a programme with these features.

6.9. We need a more intelligible range of qualifications. At present, some 3,500 vocational qualifications are available for young people to study. Many of them are essentially proprietary – known to most people according to the name of the body awarding them. Some have currency in some sectors of the economy. None are as widely understood and recognised as GCSEs and A levels – which are offered by different awarding bodies, but understood according to a recognised

Vocational routes into higher education and skilled employment

Taking the vocational route to a Cambridge education

David Eaves left his comprehensive school at 16 to do a Modern Apprenticeship and NVQs. Just seven years later, he has graduated from Cambridge with a distinction in his Master of Engineering.

David was an Apprentice at BNFL in Preston, working towards an NVQ level 3 in electrical and electronic engineering, and studying for A level maths, when he participated in the Sutton Trust Engineering Summer School at Cambridge. The experience persuaded him to apply to the university.

In October 2000, David started his degree in engineering. BNFL sponsored him during his studies and he also got a Whitworth Scholarship (a scheme for engineering undergraduates with vocational backgrounds).

"I'm living proof that you can get into Cambridge with vocational qualifications, rather than a string of A levels", he said.

Training for hotel management at Thames Valley University...

Thames Valley University (TVU), working closely with Radisson Edwardian Hotels, pioneered Foundation Degrees for the hospitality sector, targeted at first-level managers and supervisory staff. Paul Clubb is one of those who has benefited.

At college, Paul achieved GNVQ and AVCE qualifications. He went on to complete a Pathway to Business Certificate at London Metropolitan University.

At 19, Paul decided to make the step into higher education, combining his studies with his work as a management trainee at The Ritz, in London. Paul is currently at TVU studying for a Foundation Degree in Hospitality Management. His course offers him the knowledge and experience vital to succeed in the hospitality industry. He now has career prospects as a hotel manager and is considering converting his degree to an MA in Hospitality Management at TVU.

... and for personal trainers and gym instructors at Leeds Metropolitan University

Leeds Metropolitan University's Carnegie Faculty of Sport and Education offers a Foundation Degree in Health-Related Exercise and Fitness tailored to the needs of vocational and work-based learners. Working with SkillsActive, the Sector Skills Council, Leeds Met offers progression to Foundation Degrees for Apprentices studying NVQ level 3s. The university says that these learners' qualifications have equal value to more traditional qualifications – NVQs are "just a different way of performing".

standard. We need the same recognition and understanding for vocational qualifications.

6.10. We also need to improve progression routes. At present, there are too many dead-ends, where a young person may succeed in achieving a qualification, but have no natural next step in learning. We need real pathways, in which achievement at one level prepares a young person fully to begin to work at the next and where putting together a programme which secures that result is straightforward. It is critical that these pathways are designed to ensure that young people can reach advanced level (level 3) eventually, whatever their starting point at 14.

We will create a new system of Diplomas

6.11. In achieving these objectives, we believe that the Working Group on 14-19 Reform's proposals for specialised Diplomas in vocational areas are right. We will rationalise the existing very wide array of 3,500 vocational qualifications available to young people into much more easily recognisable and understandable Diplomas, containing both specialised material and GCSEs and A levels. These Diplomas will be available at levels 1 (foundation), 2 (GCSE) and 3 (advanced). As proposed by the Working Group, they will be available in a full range of 'lines of learning', covering all the main occupational sectors of the economy.

6.12. English and maths will be included in every Diploma, because we know that they are crucial to young people's life chances. In order to achieve a level 2 Diploma, young people must achieve level 2 (GCSE level) in functional English and maths.

6.13. Crucially, we intend to put employers in the driving seat, so that they will have a key role in determining what the 'lines of learning' should be and in deciding in detail what the Diplomas should contain. That is essential, because these qualifications will only have real value to young people if they are valued by employers. We will therefore put the Sector Skills Councils (SSCs) in the lead.

6.14. HE institutions will also have an important role, because we need to be absolutely confident that a specialised level 3 Diploma can be a good route to higher education. If high achieving young people can gain access to the university of their choice by doing well in a level 3 Diploma, then once again, that will contribute to making the Diplomas a valued choice. We will therefore ask QCA to work with SSCs and HE to support the design of the Diplomas.

6.15. Qualifications reform is not a quick fix. Nor will reforming the qualifications alone solve the problems. It must be accompanied by a relentless focus on delivery in practice, on standards of provision, on engaging employers and HE in the task and on ensuring that what is on offer carries real credibility with everyone involved. It will take 10 years. But when it is done, aspiration and opportunity in this country will have been transformed for ever. We set out our detailed plans for the new system of specialised Diplomas in Chapter 7.

6.16. We will also introduce a general (GCSE) Diploma, which would recognise all young people who achieve the equivalent of 5 A*-C grade GCSEs including English and maths. We are clear that as we recognise achievement in an increasingly wide range of qualifications, we should encourage young people and schools more strongly to achieve well in English and maths, and set out in Chapter 5 our proposals for doing so. The general (GCSE) Diploma provides recognition of young people's achievement when they succeed in reaching that level.

6.17. We recognise that through this White Paper we are raising the bar through the Diploma. We have previously sought to encourage young people to achieve any 5 GCSEs or equivalent at grade C or above. In future, we will encourage them to ensure that this 5 includes English and maths – because we know that this has a significant impact on their life chances.

6.18. There are those who argue that we should challenge our A level students further by demanding breadth in the curriculum as well as stretch. We understand and appreciate these arguements, but there is no clear consensus amongst pupils, parents, employers or universities on whether or how it should be done. We also believe that so soon after Curriculum 2000, stability is important.

6.19. In the short term, we will be piloting new ways of stretching students at advanced level. We will also examine the positive experience of schools which are offering students the opportunity to take the International Baccalaureate as a means of increasing the breadth of study.

6.20. In the light of these developments, we will discuss with employers and universities whether their needs are being met and the case for introducing greater challenge and breadth alongside A levels. We will review progress in 2008.

There will be movement between routes

6.21. While it will be an essential design principle of the Diploma system that achievement at one level is a full preparation to work towards the next level, it is equally important that young people do not narrow down their choices too early. We will therefore ensure: first, that young people continue with a broad programme of study between 14 and 16, including the National Curriculum (taking up around half of their time); second, that young people who are taking GCSEs and A levels can experience some vocational learning, just as those pursuing specialised Diplomas will have a mix; and third, that it will be entirely possible to progress, for example, from a level 2 Diploma to A levels or from GCSEs to a level 3 Diploma.

All qualifications will offer stretch, young people will take them when they are ready and the expectation of leaving learning at 16 will end

6.22. At present, virtually all young people take GCSEs at the end of year 11, making the age of 16 a key moment in almost all young people's educational careers. At the moment, stretch comes mainly from taking large numbers of GCSEs. On average, young people take 8 GCSEs, but over 25% achieve 10 or more passes. Where this increases breadth, it can be highly valuable. Sometimes, however, it involves young people taking several very similar qualifications. We need to make sure that young people can stretch themselves in other ways, such as accelerating to achieve level 2 qualifications and starting advanced level study early or through enrichment activities.

6.23. In future, as we build the 14-19 phase, 16 will no longer be a fixed point in the system. Those who are capable of doing so will accelerate, moving on to advanced level study by the time they are 16. Others will take longer to get to level 2, and thereby reach a higher standard. Some of those will have succeeded in qualifications at level 1 along the way.

6.24. Whatever qualifications young people are pursuing, they should be stretched and challenged to do their best. There will be equal scope for stretch in GCSEs and in specialised level 2 Diplomas. Drawing on the lessons from KS3, the Secondary National Strategy will support schools to accelerate more young people through to GCSE or to level 2 vocational qualifications, where they are capable of succeeding early. We will remove any barriers to acceleration, and ensure that performance tables and the inspection framework recognise accelerated achievement, as set out in Chapter 12.

Accelerated French in Coventry

Take up of languages at advanced level in Coventry is low and French teachers are keen to increase the numbers progressing to that level. They have focused on accelerating gifted and talented linguists through GCSE to start AS level early.

The programme began in September 2003 with students from four schools attending a twilight class weekly for an hour and a half. This was supplemented during the year with holiday schools and revision seminars at Warwick University.

At the end of year 10, all the students participating achieved grade C or better in GCSE French, with most achieving A and B grades. Many of the students progressed to AS level French in year 11, while others chose to take an additional GCSE in Spanish. At least half of the students have said that they expect to continue studying one or more languages at advanced level post-16.

6.25. For those who do accelerate, we will make it easier to begin advanced level study. Some students may take only one or two units and would be able to bank these towards the achievement of A levels or a level 3 Diploma post-16. Others may take whole AS or equivalent qualifications in year 11 and their achievement will be recognised in performance tables. We will ensure through the Secondary National Strategy that 11-16 schools are supported to do this, including by working with other schools where necessary.

6.26. The tailored system we seek to create will challenge young people to achieve success as soon as they are able. The New Relationship with Schools and the accountability arrangements associated with it will ensure that schools have incentives to do so; and the Secondary National Strategy will support them in making a success of it. However, we will also recognise the achievement of those young people who do succeed in qualifications having taken a little longer to do so. We are undertaking work to look at adapting the performance tables to reflect this.

Chapter 7
A new system of Diplomas

Summary

In order to support the creation of the new, tailored 14-19 phase, we will introduce a new system of employer-designed Diplomas.

- To achieve a Diploma, young people will need to achieve appropriate standards in English and maths, specialised content relevant to the Diploma line, relevant GCSEs and A levels and work experience.

- We will introduce the Diplomas in 14 lines and make these a national entitlement by 2015, with four lines available by 2008 and a further four by 2010.

- We will work with employers to offer more opportunities to young people to learn at work and outside school.

- We will continue to improve the quality and broaden the reach of employment-based training through Apprenticeships, which will come within the Diploma framework.

7.1. We have set out in Chapter 6 our plans for introducing a new system of specialised Diplomas which will underpin the new, more personalised 14-19 phase. In this Chapter we set out more detail of our plans for the design and delivery of the Diplomas.

7.2. We will specify the broad areas which will make up the Diploma. In order to complete any Diploma, a young person will need to demonstrate at the appropriate level:

- a core of functional skills in English and maths;

- specialised learning in the relevant discipline;

- suitable work experience; and

- any relevant GCSEs or A levels (for example, science necessary for understanding engineering).

7.3. We will ask QCA to work with employers to devise a set of national standards, tied to international benchmarks, which will apply to all Diplomas. They will set out what every Diploma must contain.

7.4. We expect that, at the outset, Diplomas will be constructed largely out of existing qualifications and units of qualifications. Within each, there will be options, but we need to have confidence that the combination of units taken really does provide the sort of preparation that employers and universities are looking for. Therefore, there will be strict rules about which combinations will count. Over time, we expect new qualifications and units to be commissioned as part of the process of keeping Diplomas up to date.

Illustration of how the system will work – David

At KS3, David achieved National Curriculum level 6s in English and science and a 7 in maths – putting him firmly in the upper quartile of performers. As someone who is not only academically able but also enjoys taking things apart and putting them back together again, he had a particular interest in engineering.

He considered two routes in KS4:

- A straight GCSE route. On this route, he might take maths, English language and literature, ICT, double science, history, French and a new GCSE in engineering. As maths is a strength, he might take GCSE early and progress on to AS by 16.

- A mixed route including an engineering level 2 Diploma. At the end of this Chapter, we illustrate using existing qualifications what such a Diploma might look like. David might take GCSEs in maths, English language and literature and ICT. As before, he might take maths early and go on to AS. He might also do a further GCSE outside his Diploma – say, French. Then, to achieve the Diploma, he might take GCSE double award applied science, GCSE design technology and a BTEC First Certificate in engineering. He would also have optional modules available to him drawn from other GCSEs, such as electronics and qualifications which require him to apply his learning, such as City and Guilds progression awards and NVQs.

On either route, David would have a further choice at 16. He might consider:

- Doing A levels.

- Doing a level 3 Diploma. The Diploma might include A level maths, a double award vocational A level or a BTEC certificate in engineering, and other options, which might include AS level physics and design and technology and applied ICT qualifications.

On either route, he might undertake an extended project. It could take a range of forms – designing and building a machine might fit better with the Diploma combination; something more theoretical with the A level option. There would also be other stretching options on both routes – for example pulling down an HE module from an engineering degree.

On both of these routes, he would be well prepared for university – not only in engineering, but in a range of other HE options as well.

This example demonstrates both a vocational programme with significant academic content and a stretching programme for a high achiever. It also shows that it is possible to pursue some vocational learning on the 'academic' route; and substantial academic learning on the 'vocational' route.

Preparation for the motor vehicle industry in Nottingham

The motor industry offers many opportunities to young people in the Nottingham area, yet 60% of those starting training post-16 were dropping out. The City of Nottingham 14-19 pathfinder built a partnership between EMTEC (a training organisation), Toyota UK, the Institute of Motor Industry (IMI), LSC Nottinghamshire and Djanogly City Academy to design a scheme to address the problem by getting students interested in the industry earlier.

The scheme complements the students' GCSE studies and leads to a national pre-Apprenticeship qualification. Successful young people can subsequently 'fast track' on to a full Apprenticeship programme at 16 with EMTEC, or take up the opportunity to go on to an Apprenticeship programme with a local dealership.

At the end of their second year, all the students involved in the initial pilot gained their IMI level 1 qualification in light vehicle maintenance and repair. Twelve students also achieved a level 2 qualification.

For Laura Knight, the course has been valuable in helping her make up her mind about her future career. "I have always wanted to join the army and service tanks, either straight after A levels or after university," says Laura. "This course has made me even more determined to do this. It has been great to have the chance to start learning these technical skills two years earlier than normal."

7.5. Choices within the Diplomas would include options for specialisation. As young people progress through the system and become clearer about what they want to do, they may specialise in a particular occupation. The range of specialised options within a Diploma might be quite broad and this would clearly need to be recognised in the title of the Diploma.

7.6. The qualifications that will be available to young people in future will be GCSEs, A levels and Apprenticeships and those that fall within one of the lines of the Diploma. We will progressively move to a position where we fund only those qualifications consistent with the programmes and Diplomas described in this document.

Designing the Diploma

7.7. Subject to consultation, we set out in Table 7.1 our initial views on what we think the lines should be. In each line, we will ask one or more of the SSCs to take the lead in deciding with QCA what should be contained within the specialised lines and what the detailed requirements should be.

7.8. We would expect that as SSCs design these Diplomas, they will often include at least some GCSEs and A levels among the requirements. The new GCSEs in vocational subjects would be prominent among these, as would vocational A levels. In engineering, for example, a young person preparing for university entry might well take A level maths and some physical science in pursuing a level 3 Diploma. Often, communication skills in other languages will be important.

7.9. However, the details of what will be included will be something to be determined by the SSCs, working with QCA and the other key bodies. They will determine what young people will need in order to get a good preparation for employment, further study and specialisation. In virtually all lines, we will expect that there will be real stretch in the advanced level Diploma for those preparing for admission to a top university.

Table 7.1: Specialised learning lines

Specialised learning line	Relevant Sector Skills Councils
1 Health and social care	Skills for Health Skills for Care and Development
2 Public services	Central Government Skills for Justice
3 Land based and environmental	Lantra
4 Engineering	SEMTA Go Skills Energy & Utility Skills Cogent
5 Manufacturing	Skillfast-UK ProSkills SEMTA Improve
6 Construction and the built environment	Construction Skills Summit Skills Asset Skills Energy & Utility Skills
7 Information and communication technology	e-skills UK
8 Retail	Skillsmart Skills for Logistics Automotive Skills Go Skills
9 Hospitality and catering	People 1st
10 Hair and beauty	People 1st SkillsActive
11 Sport and leisure	SkillsActive
12 Travel and tourism	People 1st
13 Creative and media	Creative and Cultural Skills Skillset
14 Business administration and finance	Financial Services Sector Council

Progression

7.10. It will be a principle of the design of these Diplomas that achievement at one level is a full preparation to begin to work towards the next level. In addition, we want the design of Diplomas to encourage young people to move on from one level to the next. The most obvious route for achieving this is the one proposed by the Working Group on 14-19 Reform – that the Diplomas should interlock, so that some of what is achieved at one level counts towards what is needed at the next.

7.11. In addition, we expect achievement of the Diploma to provide a sound foundation for continuing in the education and training system through other routes. Particularly at Key Stage 4, the educational experience of young people will remain a broad preparation for life as well as work. All 14-16 year-olds will still pursue the full National Curriculum, even if they are also working towards the Diploma, and so will be preparing themselves for a range of options post-16. For example, young people achieving the level 2 Diploma during the course of KS4, along with other GCSEs, should be well prepared to move onto a work-based route through Apprenticeship or on to an A level route as well as to progress on to a level 3 Diploma and then into HE.

7.12. In addition, we will ensure that young people who achieve part of their Diploma can carry on to complete it as adults, taking with them the units and qualifications they have achieved in the 14-19 phase. The design of the Diplomas will therefore fit very closely with the adult qualifications framework. Depending on the outcome of the consultation on the Framework for Achievement for adult qualifications, it may be used as the basis for constructing Diplomas. Of course, only a proportion of the qualifications and units that will be included in the Framework will be available to young people. But we will ensure that vocational units and qualifications taken by young people will also be available to them as adults.

7.13. We want to work with the HE sector to ensure that diplomas provide a route into HE. We will involve the sector in the design of the diplomas, to ensure that they provide a proper preparation for study at university level. Universities and other HE providers will need to ensure that their admissions procedures can fairly assess young people who follow the Diploma route.

The role of employers in delivering the Diploma

7.14. Much of the extended vocational provision will be provided by schools directly, for example by Specialist Schools as part of their specialism, making their specialist provision and facilities available to other schools as appropriate. We are clear that the content of the specialised lines needs to offer

---

Illustration of how the new system will work – Tina

Tina achieved National Curriculum level 5 in English, maths and science at 14. Her school considered her to be an able student who was not fully displaying her abilities. She had a particular interest in creative and new technologies. She considered taking a range of GCSEs, including art and design, drama and ICT. However, she decided that the level 2 Diploma would be the better route for her: so alongside the core of the National Curriculum, she took applied GCSE art and design with a vocational qualification in IT, through which she learned how to use and apply new information and communication technologies to a variety of real workplace challenges – partly through time in college but also on a work placement in a local graphic design business. Because she became so enthused by the possibilities of pursuing her studies in this area further, she re-doubled her efforts in the core of the National Curriculum and scored more highly there than the school expected.

Consequently, at 16, she was well prepared for a further choice of which route to pursue. Options might include an Apprenticeship, building on her experiences in the workplace at KS4; a level 3 Diploma in the same field (which might encompass A level art and design and a vocational qualification in media plus AS business studies and specialist units in new media skills); a level 3 Diploma in a different field; or A levels.

This example shows how someone achieving in the mid-range of performance in academic subjects but with a desire to pursue more strongly a specific interest or with a preference for more practical learning might receive a boost to their motivation and engagement through a more tailored experience. Tina would currently find it very difficult to pursue her particular interest pre-16. Consequently, not only would she be less well prepared to pursue that interest post-16, but also she would not receive the boost to her engagement in other subjects.

a range of different learning styles. For example, on a catering course:

- you might learn how to cook in a professional setting, not just about how catering is done;

- the course is delivered by people who have real workplace experience and expertise as well as teaching skills – chefs, not cookery teachers; and

- it is delivered in a proper professional environment – in the sort of kitchen that would be found in a restaurant.

7.15. Of course, this can be delivered in an educational establishment as well as in a workplace. And, in fact, because some colleges have restaurants, farms, hairdressers and so on, the college environment can itself be a work environment. However, for many young people, real contact with real employers is an important motivation. And for employers – especially those facing skills shortages – it provides a means to train and attract the next generation of skilled employees.

7.16. We therefore want to challenge employers to become more involved in providing opportunities to learn in a work setting. We know from the early success of the Young Apprenticeship programme that many employers are able to make a serious contribution to supporting young people to

learn. We want to ensure that every young person pursuing a vocational route has some good quality engagement with employers. And we want to ensure that girls and boys are not constrained in their choices by outmoded ideas of what are male or female occupations.

7.17. Quite how much employer engagement there is will of course depend on employers – both on the local employment market and on employers' willingness to get involved. In reality, there will be a continuum – with the Young Apprenticeship model, of 50 days learning alongside skilled workers with an employer, being at the higher end. Young Apprenticeships will be one important way in which 14-16 year-olds will pursue the new Diplomas.

7.18. How much time young people will spend with an employer will depend on a range of factors:

- the nature of the qualifications being undertaken. Some qualifications require real, practical, work-based training, while others (for example, ICT qualifications which focus on programming) do not;

Young Apprenticeship – STEPs into Health and Social Care

The STEPs Young Apprenticeship programme in Northumberland prepares young people for careers within the health and social care sector. Currently, 30 young people are engaged on the programme from two schools, Ashington Community High School and Cramlington Community High School. The employer partners are Northumbria Healthcare NHS Trust and Northumberland Care Trust.

Each Young Apprentice's programme is based on an individual learning plan. All are studying for the dual award GCSE in Health and Social Care, brought to life through work placements and speakers from the NHS and social care sector. The work placements, offered on a weekly basis during term time, provide Young Apprentices with opportunities to work in a wide variety of settings within the primary and acute health services and the social care sector. Each Young Apprentice is guided in their work placement activities by a workplace supervisor.

One Young Apprentice, Michelle Wandless, said, "cardiology was very interesting. I found out lots of new things, such as how the ward was run and in what order things had to be done. I'm looking forward to my next placement."

- the likely motivational and achievement gains from spending time with an employer. For example, a young person who could get to the equivalent of 5 GCSEs at A*-C grade by the age of 16 by spending time with an employer, but who might otherwise be likely to miss out, would be a real priority; and

- what the young person is likely to do next. A 14-16 year-old planning to go on to an Apprenticeship or other work-based training would be very likely to benefit from an extended period with an employer. Someone planning to continue on an A level route might benefit more from time with an employer later on.

7.19. However, all young people on a vocational route will have a significantly different learning experience from a purely classroom-based one. And all young people will be undertaking work-related learning.

Apprenticeships provide the employment-based route

7.20. The Apprenticeship programme provides employment-based training for 16-24 year-olds. In 2004/5, about quarter of a million young people were pursuing an Apprenticeship and some 130,000 employers were involved. Apprentices are employees who are learning on the job. They will generally be looking to achieve an NVQ in the relevant occupational area (at level 3 if they are pursuing an Advanced Apprenticeship and at level 2 otherwise), a technical certificate and Key Skills qualifications.

7.21. Our target this year is for 28% of 16-21 year-olds to start an Apprenticeship – some 175,000 young people. The Cassels Committee, which reviewed Apprenticeships, proposed as a target that 35% should start an Apprenticeship by 2010 – taking us to the average for North West Europe.

7.22. Getting a place on an Apprenticeship is competitive. Employers naturally want to employ the right people for their business. Completing an Apprenticeship is demanding.

Young people need to be able to juggle the rigours of the workplace with achieving their qualifications. And those who have completed their Apprenticeships are highly prized by employers.

7.23. Issues remain. We will be expanding the number of Apprenticeships. At the same time, we are aiming to make sure that every Apprenticeship is as good as the majority already are – driving up quality. And we are seeking to ensure that completion rates are pushed up. Even in those cases where a young person is promoted early or moved to another employer, we want to encourage them to complete their Apprenticeship, because we believe that doing so has long-term benefits for them. We will challenge traditional stereotypes and through high-quality advice and guidance encourage young people to consider all types of Apprenticeship regardless of their gender, ethnicity, background or any disabilities. Breaking down gender stereotypes could help to address skills shortages in, for example, construction or plumbing.

7.24. Apprenticeships are a well understood and widely recognised brand. We do not want to make significant further changes beyond those already outlined. However, we do want to make sure that there is proper integration between our proposals for the Diploma and the existing Apprenticeship framework. Already, the Apprenticeship has the features that we have said should characterise the Diploma – a core of functional skills, significant vocational content, relevant academic content – and its design is employer-led. The major difference, of course, is that the young person following an Apprenticeship is in employment. This means that, while the course of learning a young person is following may be very different, the qualification which results is not. We therefore wish to integrate Apprenticeships within the Diploma framework, in much the way the Working Group on 14-19 Reform recommended, so that Apprentices can achieve the Diploma.

Illustration of how the new system will work – Katharine

Katharine achieved National Curriculum level 4s in English, maths and science at 14. Recognising her need for additional support in the basics, her school offered her a focused package of curriculum support in functional English and maths, intended to achieve the result that in the functional skills she would achieve level 2 by 16. At the same time, she began work towards a level 1 Diploma in travel and tourism, building on her interests in travel. With the chance to study in a more practical way and a day each week in a travel agency, which showed her how what she was learning was useful in practice, she felt for the first time that she was succeeding in learning. She successfully completed the vocational elements of her level 1 Diploma at the end of year 10. With that achieved, she was keen to carry on to work towards level 2 from year 11 onwards. At the end of year 11, she was able to succeed in achieving level 2 functional English and maths. She is now working towards completing her level 2 Diploma in travel and tourism at the college where she had been studying part-time.

Katharine's attainment at 14 is in the lowest 7% nationally of those taking KS3 tests. Almost no-one gets 5 A*-C GCSEs at 16 from that starting point (6%) – those that do predominantly have English as an additional language – so that lack of language competence at 14 disguises ability in other subjects. However, the vast majority of the group do go on to study for GCSEs, where they score poorly. Having done so, their onward progression route is very unclear (retakes having very low success rates). Very many are then outside learning post-16. Under the new system, Katharine does not reach level 2 by 16, but she does achieve success in a qualification which can take her on to success at level 2 a little later.

Delivering the Diploma

7.25. It will be a national entitlement that every young person will have access to each of the lines of the Diploma. This will take time. The full entitlement will be in place nationally by 2015. The first four lines will be available by 2008, covering ICT; engineering; health and social care; and creative and media. There will be a further four lines by 2010, including construction. We will be working with the relevant SSCs named in Table 7.1 and with relevant professional bodies, HE institutions and awarding bodies to develop, pilot and then make widely available these new qualifications.

7.26. This does not, of course, mean that we expect every school and college to offer all of these lines. That would be unrealistic and undeliverable. However, we do expect that each young person will have access to each of the lines within a reasonable distance of home. In every area, providers will ensure that between them they are making a full offer to young people.

7.27. We also expect that in each area, each line will offer good quality teaching, training and learning. Already, the 'Success for All' programme has developed new teaching and learning and support strategies for vocational education. We will build on these in order to ensure that all young people receive good quality education and training.

Specialised Diplomas – Illustrations

Note: It will be SSCs who will lead the design of the specialised Diplomas. The following tables illustrate, using existing qualifications, how the Diplomas might be constructed. These examples relate to existing qualifications which, over time, may change according to employer and HE requirements.

Diploma in Engineering

Level	Age	Core			Main vocational learning			Optional specialised units taken from within...		
Intermediate	14-17	GCSE Maths	GCSE English	GCSE Applied ICT	GCSE Double Award or BTEC[1] First Certificate Engineering	GCSE Design Technology	GCSE Science	City and Guilds[2] Progression Award in Applying Engineering Principles		
								GCSE Electronics		
								EMTA[3] NVQ[4] Performing Engineering Operations		
Advanced	16-19	A Level Maths			A Level Double Award or BTEC National Certificate Engineering			AS Physics	AS Design Technology	BTEC National Award or OCR[5] Certificate for IT Practitioners

Diploma in Creative and Media

Level	Age	Core				Main vocational learning		Optional specialised units taken from within...		
Intermediate	14-17	GCSE Maths	GCSE English	ICT Key Skills	GCSE Science	Applied GCSE Art and Design	OCR Level 2 National Certificate in IT or BTEC First Diploma for IT Practitioners	GCSE Spanish	GCSE Film Studies	BTEC First Certificate in Media
Advanced	16-19	A Level Art and Design				BTEC National Certificate in Media or OCR National Diploma in Media		AS Business studies	ABC[6] Award in Online Media Production Skills	City and Guilds Diploma in Media Techniques

The award of a Diploma will require the achievement of a minimum volume of qualifications – for example at intermediate, the qualifications achieved must be equivalent to a minimum 5 A*-C at GCSE and include functional English and maths. The relevant SSCs and HE institutions may determine content which is greater than the national minimum.

[1] BTEC is a qualification brand.
[2] City and Guilds is an awarding body.
[3] EMTA Awards Limited is the industry awarding body for engineering and technology.
[4] National Vocational Qualification.
[5] Oxford, Cambridge and RSA Examinations is an awarding body.
[6] Awarding Body Consortium (ABC) is an awarding body.

Chapter 8
Strengthening GCSEs and A levels

Summary

We will keep both GCSEs and A levels, but improve both. At GCSE we will:

- restructure English and maths GCSEs to make sure it is impossible to get a grade C or above without functional English and maths, as described in Chapter 5;

- review coursework to reduce the assessment burden;

- continue work to reform maths as proposed by Professor Adrian Smith, improving motivation and progression to advanced level. This is likely to include a new double maths GCSE; and

- continue to promote science – including implementing the new science GCSEs – restating our firm expectation that young people should do two science GCSEs.

At A level we will:

- increase stretch for the most able by introducing harder, Advanced Extension Award (AEA)-style questions into separate sections at the end of A level papers;

- introduce the 'extended project' to stretch all young people and test a wider range of higher-level skills;

- enable young people to take HE modules while in the sixth form;

- ensure that universities have more information on which to make judgements about candidates by ensuring that they have access to the grades achieved by young people in individual modules. We will also support those universities who wish to have marks as well as grades; and

- we will reduce the assessment burden at A level by reducing the expectation of numbers of assessments in an A level from 6 to 4 – but without any change in the overall content of A levels.

We will ensure that there are natural progression routes both through the levels of the Diploma and between GCSEs and A levels and the different levels of the Diploma. By doing so, we will secure for all young people routes that avoid early narrowing down, but provide them with real choice of what to learn and in what setting.

We will strengthen GCSEs

8.1. The GCSE is an internationally known and respected qualification. We believe that having a single qualification available to the whole cohort has significant strengths, as compared, for example, to the previous CSE/O level system, where young people were assigned to a particular level at 14. We will preserve and strengthen it in the new system.

GCSE English and maths

8.2. It is vital that all young people are able to use English and maths in practice. We said in Chapter 5 that GCSEs in English and maths should be revised to ensure that students cannot get a grade C or better without passing (by reaching a high threshold) a functional skills unit. Those who pass the functional element without succeeding in the GCSE will have their achievement in the functional unit separately recognised.

8.3. Changes to GCSE maths will happen within the context of work already underway in response to Professor Adrian Smith's report, 'Making Mathematics Count'. The package of changes to GCSE maths arising from this work is intended to raise achievement in maths and lead to more students taking maths at advanced level and beyond. It includes:

- development of a two-tier GCSE which will mean that no-one walks into the exam room knowing that a grade C is impossible; and no-one gets a B or above without being assessed on the most testing parts of the syllabus;

- a review of the content and size of GCSE maths, including the role of ICT in the curriculum, teaching and learning, and assessment, and the content and teaching of statistics and data-handling; and

- development of a curriculum and assessment model for maths provision setting out clear pathways from National Qualifications Framework (NQF) entry level to level 3.

8.4. There are no similar issues affecting the redesign of GCSE English. We do not therefore expect extensive change beyond what is necessary to secure functional English. In particular, GCSE English will continue to require the reading of a range of texts, including Shakespeare.

Science

8.5. We set out in Chapter 5 the improvements we have made with the science community in the KS4 syllabus. New GCSEs have been successfully piloted and will be fully available for 2006. It is our firm expectation that students should continue to do two science GCSEs. Science will continue to be compulsory at KS4 and all young people will have an entitlement to follow a course that leads to the equivalent of two science GCSEs. We will monitor the impact of the new KS4 programme of study carefully to ensure that the number of students doing at least two science GCSEs does not fall below the current 80% and that the number of young people taking science post-16 increases in line with the aspirations set out in the Government's '10 Year Investment Framework for Science and Innovation'.

Progression

8.6. Some students find modular qualifications motivating. Taking small units with assessment at the end gives students short-term targets and feedback on their learning. They can build this towards a full qualification. This can help students to accelerate, or allow them to build up more slowly to achieve a higher standard.

8.7. We do not propose to unitise all GCSEs, but will continue with developments already in hand. The new GCSEs in applied subjects launched in 2002 each comprise 3 units; and QCA is currently working with awarding bodies to develop GCSEs which contain a common core, but then a choice of general or vocational options within them. In piloting these new GCSEs, QCA should evaluate their effectiveness in helping learners to progress to level 2 achievement. GCSEs of this sort are being piloted for science and history. We believe that the extended range of GCSEs available will improve motivation and so achievement. The choice on offer, both of GCSEs and units within them, will offer greater flexibility and personalisation, enabling young people to pursue their interests within a structure that challenges them.

Enrichment

8.8. Alongside opportunities for greater stretch and challenge, we believe that all young people benefit from learning opportunities outside the formal curriculum. All young people will have the opportunity to participate in a range of sport and other activities. Some of these may take place within curriculum time, but many will not. We will set out details in due course.

Reducing assessment

8.9. Giving young people the opportunity to stretch themselves through acceleration to advanced level may reduce the number of examinations that they take overall. In addition, we think that there is scope to lessen the coursework burden, particularly by reducing it where the same knowledge and skills can be tested reliably in other ways.

8.10. The original concept of coursework was that it should be the assessment of work which would need to be done anyway as part of the course. In many subjects coursework remains an important way of testing skills that are not easily assessed in an exam, such as science experiments or performance in music. Too often, though, as the Working Group on 14-19 Reform point out, young people must complete several similar pieces of coursework in different subjects, as 'add-ons' which test similar skills to the same deadlines.

8.11. We will therefore ask QCA to undertake a review to address three principal concerns. First, we want to ensure that the approach to coursework in similar subjects is consistent and that it tests skills and attributes that cannot be tested by a terminal examination. Second, the review should address concerns about fairness. Finally, we want to address the cumulative burden of coursework. We are concerned that the overall burden on students is too high even if coursework requirements subject by subject are sensible when considered in isolation.

8.12. The review should ensure that coursework adheres to the principles of assessment set out in Chapter 9. In particular it must accurately assess what it is trying to assess, lead to the same marks being awarded for the same performance, and be fair. This means that:

- coursework should be used where it is the most valid way of assessing subject-specific skills;

- coursework should not stand alone, but should be embedded within the course as part of teaching knowledge and skills within the syllabus;

- coursework is not favoured where its primary purpose is to assess knowledge and skills which can equally well be assessed in other ways;

- coursework must be robust – including by comprising examples of work produced in lesson time, for example. 'Classwork' in this sense should be as important a concept as coursework;

- coursework requirements should be consistent, ensuring that similar subjects have similar coursework requirements; and

- the overall burden of externally set and moderated coursework across a programme should be reduced.

We will strengthen A levels

8.13. A levels allow students to pursue subjects in depth and to develop independent learning skills. They offer a clear route to HE or to employment and are a significant qualification in their own right, recognising a wide range of advanced achievement. The Curriculum 2000 reforms made A level broader and more flexible by introducing the Advanced Subsidiary GCE (AS) and establishing A levels in vocational subjects. Many candidates now do 4 AS levels (excluding general studies) in year 12, and 3 A2s in year 13 (excluding general studies). Nonetheless fewer than 40% of the age cohort take even one A level and only just over one third pass two or more.

Greater stretch and challenge at advanced level

8.14. In 2004, around 3.5% of the age cohort achieved 3 or more A grades at A level. We believe that there is more that we can do to stretch and challenge our brightest students. We also want to help universities to differentiate between the highest performing candidates.

8.15. First, we want more stretch within A levels. Because we make it a priority to preserve A level as a qualification, with consistent standards over time, we will take a slightly different route to that proposed by the Working Group. We will seek the introduction of a new section in A level papers covering AEA material. We will ask QCA to consider the best means of doing this across all A levels,

so that increased stretch and challenge are available to all students in all types of institution, and scholarship can flourish.

8.16. Second, we will follow the Working Group proposal to develop an extended project at advanced level. This will be a single piece of work, requiring a high degree of planning, preparation, research and autonomous working. The projects that students complete will differ by subject, but all will require persistence over time and research skills to explore a subject independently in real depth. We expect that students would normally complete an extended project instead of a fourth or fifth AS level.

8.17. We will ask QCA to pilot the extended project, and assess manageability for institutions. We will ask them to develop, in consultation with employers and HE, an overarching framework and detailed specifications for different types of project. In doing so, they should draw on experience of existing qualifications, such as the International Baccalaureate extended essay.

8.18. We want to ensure that there is as much scope for stretch for students pursuing a level 3 Diploma. We will ensure that the extended project is available on specialised routes. Existing vocational qualifications, such as BTEC Nationals, include an extended project as a matter of course and an extended project could be made a requirement on some Diploma lines. Equally, we ask SSCs to ensure that there are options on specialised Diplomas which, like the inclusion of AEA questions, offer greater stretch within individual components of the Diploma. In some cases this will happen automatically, through the inclusion of a requirement for A level study to achieve the Diploma.

8.19. Subject to Parliamentary approval, changes being introduced in the current Education Bill will make it lawful for schools to offer HE modules. Further education can already do so. We will work with universities to find the best way of helping schools and colleges to make use of this opportunity.

Stretching students and preparing for HE in Cumbria

Young people in Cumbria are benefiting from the opportunity to sample a real university course while still at school. They choose Open University short courses from a range of options, including astronomy, life in the oceans and robotics.

In the first wave, 55 of 72 students successfully completed their courses and were awarded certificates in October 2004. The remaining 17 students may finish later this year. The certificates are worth 10 CAT points towards a related degree. More importantly, they help convince HE admissions tutors of a student's ability to be successful at university level study, demonstrating their commitment and independent learning skills.

The scheme has now been opened up more widely and 128 students have enrolled. Each student receives a distance learning pack containing all course materials and has access to an Open University subject tutor by telephone and internet conference. Schools provide a trained support teacher to monitor student progress, provide advice and meet any pastoral needs.

Once again, this is as applicable to vocational as to academic study.

Greater differentiation

8.20. When piloted and introduced nationally, these measures will help universities to differentiate between candidates. We are currently considering the implications and options for implementing a system of post-qualification application (PQA). We will be consulting on our proposals. We believe PQA will simplify and increase the fairness of the admissions procedure for young people and higher education institutions alike. PQA will be a major change to admissions procedures and is unlikely to be fully in place before 2010.

8.21. Differentiation is an issue now for some higher education institutions, who find their most popular courses oversubscribed by students predicted straight As at A level. A rapid solution to this problem ahead of implementation of the new stretching options is simply to make available to universities more information about students' performance.

8.22. We welcome the UCAS consultation on introducing information about candidates' unit grades into the system. We believe unit grades will help universities to choose between candidates on the basis of robust and objective information. We encourage UCAS

and the Joint Council for Qualifications to work together to provide the AS unit grades in time for the 2006 admissions round. Once PQA is in place, we expect all AS and A2 unit grades to be routinely available to all HE institutions. We do not want these arrangements to increase the number of re-sits taken and will ask QCA to review the rules to ensure that this does not happen. While students' UMS scores are not as directly comparable as unit grades, we are happy to support any universities which ask to see this information as well.

8.23. Research is also to be carried out on the usefulness of a single aptitude test, as recommended in the report of the Admissions to HE Steering Group (the Schwartz report).

Less assessment

8.24. We are committed to ensuring that assessment does not place undue strain on students, institutions or the system. Early concerns about the impact on assessment of Curriculum 2000 have largely subsided as the reforms have become better established, but we believe that we can do more to reduce the pressure on students, institutions and the system.

8.25. Both Sir Mike Tomlinson's 'Inquiry into A level Standards' and the final report of the Working Group proposed a reduction in the number of assessment units at A level without change to their content. We agree. Currently, most A levels have 6 units, each separately assessed and sometimes by more than one exam paper. In future, most A levels will have four larger units, covering the same amount of content, but only 4 assessments. This will reduce by a third the assessment burden. It will also reduce costs and address exam timetabling difficulties. This structure will not be appropriate in every subject and we expect it to be introduced gradually, as exams are re-accredited.

Other changes

8.26. In addition, we will ask QCA to address some specific issues that have arisen in a few subjects, where either the content is unbalanced between AS and A2 or it needs revision to reflect subject developments, or to provide better progression, for instance in history. In addition, some A level syllabuses are very similar to one another. For example, ICT and computing are separate A levels but do not have separate subject criteria. There is a need to create a clear distinction between the two and to take account of recent developments in ICT.

8.27. We have considered what scope there is to reduce coursework at A level. We are persuaded by advice from QCA that most A level coursework is subject-specific and could not be replaced by a single extended project. We will nonetheless ask QCA to consider carefully the burden of coursework in individual subjects and the cumulative effect across A level programmes when awarding bodies submit new specifications or seek re-accreditation.

Chapter 9
Engaging all young people

Summary

Many young people need additional support in order to progress during the 14-19 phase, for a wide range of reasons. For many, the new curriculum choices, including different styles and places of learning will provide them with opportunities to develop their talents and mean that they are more likely to succeed. Foundation and entry level qualifications will help more young people onto a pathway to further opportunities and qualifications.

For young people who face serious personal problems, the measures being taken as part of the 'Every Child Matters' agenda will be crucial in breaking down the barriers to achievement. In addition, we will develop a pilot programme for 14-16 year olds, based on the post-16 Entry to Employment programme as part of a coherent framework of provision below level 2. This will:

- provide a tailored programme for each young person and intensive personal guidance and support;

- involve significant work-based learning, probably amounting to two days each week;

- lead towards a level 1 Diploma; and

- lead on to a range of further options, including Apprenticeship.

9.1. Many of the proposals already set out in this White Paper are fundamentally about providing better opportunities for those who – whatever their current level of attainment – do not have the opportunities they need to make the most of themselves or to pursue their talents. However, there are some young people who face much greater barriers to learning and who are not being engaged at all in the education and training system. We need to continue to strengthen provision for those who are not offered a good curriculum and qualifications route through the 14-19 phase, those who are in the so-called 'NEET' (Not in Education, Employment or Training) group between 16 and 19 and other young people who disengage from learning during their secondary years.

Identifying those in need of more engaging opportunities

9.2. There are therefore several very different groups in need of additional support in order to make the most of the new 14-19 phase. We want to ensure that those with special educational needs have the support that they need in order to progress and achieve. We want to be sure that those at risk of disengagement are brought back into the system. And we want to be sure that young people with significant barriers to learning are supported to overcome them.

9.3. The economic and social costs of young people being in the NEET group are high and they are the young people who we most need to re-engage in education and training. At the end of 2003, around 9% of 16-18 year olds were estimated to be NEET. Only around 1% of the cohort is 'long term' NEET – in other words NEET at 16, 17 and 18 – with a further 4% in the group at two out of three of these ages.

9.4. The group is highly diverse. For example, it does not solely comprise low attainers: around 27% have high GCSE attainment. Some, we do not need to be concerned about: for example, some 15% of 18 year-old NEETs are young people on gap years. However, there is a set of risk factors that may lead to young people becoming NEET. For example, young people are more likely to be in the NEET group if they:

- have low attainment at GCSE;

- are from lower socio-economic groups;

- were persistent truants in year 11; or

- are teenage mothers.

9.5. Part of the solution will be to offer these young people qualifications and a curriculum that they want to pursue post-16. However, that is far from the whole story. We need to begin to address the reasons for their disengagement earlier in the 14-19 phase and indeed before that; and we need to address the biggest barriers to learning specifically.

Providing for all young people

9.6. We believe there are three broad groups whose particular needs should be recognised and addressed:

- students who drop out at least partly because the curriculum, qualifications or learning styles available do not motivate them;

- students whose low achievement may be due to personal problems which have nothing to do with the curriculum or qualifications on offer; and

- students with learning difficulties.

Enhancing qualifications and the curriculum

9.7. The first priority for re-engaging those who are not motivated by the school experience is to intervene as soon as problems emerge. That is why we have invested heavily in early education and in primary schools. It is also why we have invested in improving the quality of teaching and learning for 11-14 year-olds.

9.8. Through continuing this work and through the review of Key Stage 3 we are putting in place, we aim to ensure not only that more young people achieve more by the age of 14, but also that more are engaged and motivated by education at the start of the 14-19 phase. In addition, our attendance and behaviour strategies have an important role to play. We know that those who do not attend school do not achieve and are disproportionately likely to end up in the Criminal Justice System. We will continue our drive to improve attendance and behaviour in schools.

9.9. Second, our proposals to secure the basics are crucial for this group. Those who do not achieve the expected level in English and maths at 11 (National Curriculum level 4) do not have sufficiently good functional skills to access the secondary school curriculum. Similarly, those who do not achieve the expected level in the basics at 14 struggle to really benefit from education 14-16 without significant additional support. This is a major cause of disengagement, and young people achieving lower levels at 14 have less chance of getting 5 A*-C grade GCSEs or equivalent.

9.10. Third, this White Paper introduces new opportunities for young people to enjoy new styles of learning and to learn in a different setting. There will be more opportunities for practical, applied learning. There will be more opportunities to learn in a different, often more adult, environment – including the potential for a significant experience of the workplace. Equally, there will be a continued focus on improving teaching and learning – through the Secondary National Strategy and through the improvements in post-16 teaching supported

by the DfES Standards Unit as part of Success for All.

9.11. Fourth, this White Paper ensures that young people are able to pursue qualifications pitched at the right level for them, whatever that might be. QCA and the LSC already plan to develop a range of units for those working below level 2. These would cover functional skills, vocational and general learning and personal and social development. We intend that every young person should be supported and challenged to achieve the most of which they are capable. The new proposals for stretch in this White Paper achieve that for some young people; the new proposals for better progression at foundation level achieve it for others.

9.12. The new level 1 Diploma will provide a wholly new opportunity for young people to take qualifications at which they can succeed and which then prepare them to progress to the next level. As a consequence, we expect more young people to attain higher levels, by taking a little longer to get there where necessary. At the same time, the separate identification of the core of functional maths and English and the introduction of level 1 functional skills qualifications into KS4 will ensure that more young people are working at an appropriate level in the basics.

Motivating and achieving through the performing arts in Coventry

The Belgrade Acting Out project is a joint venture between Coventry local authority and the Belgrade Theatre, designed to motivate young people with attendance, behaviour and learning difficulties.

Young people from mainstream and special schools work together towards a BTEC First qualification. They spend up to a day each week off the school site and are introduced to drama, theatre production, dance and music. They create, produce, and perform their own pieces of original theatre, developed from issues affecting their lives, their interests, thoughts, ideas and feelings.

The impact on students has impressed parents and inspectors alike. HMI Clive Kempton commented, "pupils have moved a tremendous distance in confidence, self-esteem, and reformed behaviour. Some pupils spoke of how they felt different back in school". A parent reported how "the project has helped our daughter tremendously with her self-confidence, her relationships, and consideration of others".

The results are also impressive. In 2004, 22 of the 24 who started completed the course. 17 achieved a BTEC First in Performing Arts. Five pupils who attended special schools were not entered for the full qualification, but achieved parts of some units.

9.13. In addition, we will make much greater use of extra-curricular activities, through extended schools and in other ways. And we will ensure that we support schools and others to integrate the wider activities undertaken by young people back into the curriculum – so that young people's education receives the full benefit of the motivational effects.

9.14. We believe that our education system will be offering a significantly different set of opportunities to young people, which will have a real impact on tackling the progressive disengagement of some young people during secondary education.

Personal problems which stand in the way of educational success

9.15. For some young people, serious personal problems stand in the way of their educational success. In 'Every Child Matters', we set out our ambitious and comprehensive agenda for promoting the welfare of children and young people. We explained how the many problems that can affect young people can combine to reduce the life chances of some. Young people may experience a range of problems:

- some 10,000 over 16s are classed as 'looked after', as are more than 25,000 10-15 year olds;

- 17,000 16-19 year-olds are subject to supervision orders, of whom 5,000 are NEET;

- 2,500 are in custodial institutions;

- teenage pregnancy. Three-quarters of 18 year-old mothers are NEET; and

- research suggests that a significant proportion of the 'long-term' NEET have become disaffected with society and marginalised. This is frequently associated with dysfunctional family relationships, emotional or behavioural difficulties, homelessness, drug or alcohol abuse or criminal activity.

9.16. We have put in place a range of measures to tackle barriers to learning. First, the new Education Maintenance Allowances, now available across the country, are designed to ensure that young people can afford to continue in education. They provide a strong incentive to carry on for those young people who will benefit from remaining in education, but who might otherwise be tempted to leave. Evaluation of earlier pilots has shown that they increased participation in pilot areas by 5.9% and reduced the number of 16 year-olds joining the NEET group by 2.7%. The response to the consultation on 'Supporting Young People to Achieve' which will be published with the Budget for 2005 will set out our longer-term plans to ensure that all 16-19 year-olds have the financial support they need to participate in education and training.

9.17. Second, we will make sure that young people at risk receive effective targeted support to help them to overcome barriers to learning. The Connexions service has had some success in beginning to reduce the size of the NEET group. We will set out our plans for building on this to ensure that all young people have the personal support they need, in due course.

9.18. Third, within the very broad Every Child Matters programme, targeted initiatives, from the teenage pregnancy strategy through the range of behaviour support interventions to programmes to reduce the abuse of drugs and alcohol will disproportionately benefit this group of 14-19 year-olds.

9.19. Fourth, the Entry to Employment programme is an individualised work-based learning programme for those aged 16-18 who have barriers to engaging or re-engaging with learning or employment. The programme aims to support young people to progress to further learning or to employment. It offers access to entry and level 1 provision, including: functional and/or Key Skills; vocational areas; and personal and social development. It includes regular contact with Connexions Personal Advisers.

9.20. This set of measures means that we now have much stronger support in place for these young people.

Students with learning difficulties

9.21. A very different group of young people who should receive support through the 14-19 phase are those with learning difficulties. They are twice as likely as others to be NEET and around 12.5% of the NEET group have learning difficulties and disabilities. Once again, we believe that we have in place a range of measures which will make a significant difference to these young people.

9.22. First, there is an improved set of qualifications. Entry level qualifications have provided a significant step forward in motivating and encouraging young people with special educational needs. QCA is now taking forward the recommendations of their report 'An evaluation of entry level qualifications' (May 2004). They are doing so within the context of developing a coherent framework of provision below level 2 as part of the new Framework for Achievement. This will allow tailoring to individual needs through bite-sized qualification units. Pre-16, we expect personalised programmes to build on the SEN framework. In particular, we expect that those with 'spiky profiles', who may have very great strengths, are stretched with appropriate provision. The entitlement to continued study of functional English and maths post-16 for those who have not achieved level 2 will also contribute.

9.23. Second, there will be improved transition planning to build on the proposals in the SEN strategy 'Removing barriers to achievement', the Strategy Unit's 'Improving life chances of disabled people', the transition standard under the National Service Framework for Disabled Children and the transition work of the Learning Disability Partnership Boards.

9.24. Third, there will be wider opportunities to develop life skills and to achieve. We are working with the LSC, QCA and awarding bodies such as ASDAN. The LSC is

conducting a strategic review of planning and funding post-16 provision for learners with learning difficulties in order to improve quality, availability and cost-effectiveness. The review also aims to increase capacity within FE colleges and encourage greater collaboration among providers from different sectors.

9.25. Fourth, the Employment sub-group of the Learning Disability Task Force (Valuing People) will shortly be sending a report to Ministers and the Task Force with recommendations for creating greater employment opportunities for young people with learning difficulties and disabilities. We will clearly consider this sensitively and sympathetically.

A new means of re-engaging the disaffected

9.26. Some of the measures described above are relatively recently introduced policy changes. Some are ongoing strategies. Others are new measures to be introduced as part of the implementation of this White Paper. We believe that taken together, they will have a very significant impact over time.

9.27. However, we believe that there is one important additional measure that we need to take, beyond those already outlined above. The Entry to Employment route provides a motivating and engaging alternative route for those 16-19 year-olds whose attainment in education is relatively low and who are at serious risk of disaffection. But there is no comparable programme designed for 14-16 year olds.

9.28. We need a strong work-focused route designed specifically to motivate those 14-16 year-old young people who are at the most risk and who we know would be motivated by a different learning environment. These young people may include those with poor records of attendance and behaviour, who are most in need of an improved offer of this sort, but are least likely to be attractive to employers.

Illustration of how the new system will work – Mary

Towards the end of KS3, Mary became progressively disillusioned with school. Difficulties at home and a long period of illness meant that she fell behind for a time and began to cause the school some problems. At the end of KS3, her achievement was not what the school would have expected when she joined them. At a review day at the end of KS3, she sat down with her form tutor and parents and discussed what to do next.

Over the course of KS4, Mary took part in the new scheme. Through a local voluntary sector organisation she received coaching and mentoring, which helped her to think through what she wanted to do, to understand what she needed to do to get there and to build her self-confidence to do it. Her close involvement with the local college and with local employers while pursuing vocational study in health and social care has also been significant in helping her to firm up her ideas. Although it has taken her a bit longer to get there, Mary is now back on track – working towards GCSEs and a level 2 Diploma in health and social care and beginning to show again her potential.

9.29. We will therefore develop and pilot a strongly work-focused programme aimed at those with serious barriers to re-engagement. It will build on the lessons of Entry to Employment in order to secure better outcomes for this group of young people. In particular, we expect that there will be a very significant work-focused component, probably amounting to as much as two days each week. And there will be very intensive advice and support for the participants. That will include direct support in the workplace and a commitment to ensure that young people will be supported in developing the general skills, attitudes and behaviours so important to employment and progression in learning. A number of voluntary sector organisations have developed good experience of working with young people in this way and we will work with them.

9.30. The programme will be tailored to the needs of the young person. At the start of the programme, young people will set goals with their adviser, both for short-term progress during their time on the programme, but also longer term, to help them to focus on their aspirations in learning and for their career. During their time on the programme, we would expect young people to continue to follow the requirements of the Key Stage 4 curriculum, with a strong emphasis on key skills. They might work towards functional skills qualifications.

9.31. They would probably begin to work towards achieving a level 1 Diploma. Some young people might not be ready to do so and would agree a different personalised programme. Others might be higher ability students who might be capable of working at a higher level relatively soon, if their personal difficulties can be resolved. All young people on the programme would be likely to follow a personal development programme, giving them the skills they need for employment and for life. A range of progression routes, including Apprenticeship, would be possible, depending on the aptitudes and preferences of the young person.

9.32. We intend to pilot this model from 2006. We would expect to be able to make it available to up to 10,000 young people from 2007/8. Its effectiveness will be evaluated thoroughly against a range of measures including the later participation of young people in education and training and their success in achieving more highly. We will also examine the wider social benefits of the programme.

9.33. If it proves successful, we expect this to have an important role in re-engaging in education and training some of our most disaffected and least well-served young people. We expect the benefits of this to those young people and to wider society to be considerable.

Chapter 10
Rigorous assessment in which all can have confidence

Summary

We believe that the current balance between internal and external assessment is essentially the right one to secure public confidence in the examinations system. We therefore do not propose major change here.

However, we will strengthen the support for assessment at KS3 through professional development and by making available nationally a bank of optional tests; we will ask QCA to undertake a review of coursework at GCSE with a view to a reduction overall; we will reduce the expected number of assessments made in A levels from 6 to 4; and we will seek to maximise the potential of e-assessment.

10.1. Assessment is an important feature of a young person's educational experience. It both supports their learning and records what they know and can do. All assessment should be valid, reliable, fair and transparent. Valid because it is an accurate reflection of the curriculum and type of learning. Reliable because the same results are awarded for identical performance. Fair because it differentiates on the basis of what students know and can do, irrespective of other factors such as background or ethnicity. And transparent because all can understand the results and processes that generate them. It must also serve the needs of all who use the system by:

- giving students accurate and precise feedback on their achievements to enable them to make informed choices about future progression;

- giving teachers data about students' performance, so that they can help the student to progress;

- giving HE and employers accurate information about what young people know and can do, as a basis for selection and development; and

- providing a rigorous basis for the accountability system so that parents can be sure that information about schools and colleges gives an accurate picture of their performance.

10.2. We believe that current assessment arrangements are valid, reliable, fair and transparent and meet the needs of those who use them. The Independent Committee on Examination Standards concluded that, "no examination system at the school level is better managed". We do not, therefore, accept the Working Group on 14-19 Reform's proposals for radical changes to the assessment system. In particular, we do not accept the proposal for replacing existing external assessment with internal teacher assessment.

10.3. We do, however, agree with the Working Group on 14-19 Reform that more robust teacher assessment can enhance the professional judgement of teachers and contribute to better teaching and learning for young people. Formative assessment is an essential part of effective teaching at every level. We also agree that the assessment burden on students, teaching staff and the system should be reduced. This Chapter, therefore, summarises our plans for improving teacher assessment at KS3 and for reducing the assessment burden.

More robust assessment at KS3

10.4. Externally set and marked National Curriculum tests will continue in the core subjects of English, maths and science. From 2008, subject to successful piloting, we will also introduce an external online examination in ICT. The remaining foundation subjects of history, geography, citizenship, design and technology, modern foreign languages, PE, music and art and design will continue to be assessed by teachers, but we will do more to improve the effectiveness of assessment.

10.5. A focus on teacher assessment supports the professionalism of teachers – developing their skills to employ teaching strategies, curriculum and assessment to personalise education to each learner's needs and aptitudes. We will provide training and guidance for teaching staff to develop their assessment skills and provide them with materials to help them to accurately assess student performance. This will include a bank of nationally-developed standardised tests and activities, which teachers can use to support their professional judgement.

Labour-market recognised qualifications 14-19

10.6. Assessment methods within qualifications differ, depending on the nature of the qualification. Most qualifications combine internal and external assessment, but in different proportions. We do not propose to alter significantly the balance between internal and external assessment in any qualification.

10.7. Where qualifications require the demonstration of practical skills, or competence in a work-related setting, they will continue to be assessed using a blend of internal and external assessment appropriate to the subject content. There are already rigorous arrangements in place to ensure that internal assessment in vocational qualifications is valid, reliable and fair. It is conducted by approved assessors, working in quality-assured centres of learning, and is supplemented by external validation, verification and moderation by representatives of the awarding body. The awarding body monitors the performance of each subject area in each centre of learning to ensure consistency of standards and practice. Assessment of the new Diplomas will be to internationally recognised standards.

10.8. In an increasingly globalised labour market, it is vital that qualifications and skills are internationally recognised and understood. As the UK takes the presidency of the EU later this year, we will pursue the development of a European Qualifications Framework and a European Credit Transfer system for vocational training to build on the existing NARIC and NRP systems. This framework will make clear for individuals, employers and providers how qualifications in England relate to those in other EU countries. We will also continue to support and promote the Europass, launched in January this year, which provides a standardised portfolio of documents for learners to use to record their qualifications and competences, including relevant work experience, in a way which can be easily understood throughout Europe.

Cutting the assessment burden at 16 and 18

10.9. We do want to cut the overall burden of assessment. The changes set out in Chapter 8 to A level and GCSE will contribute to a reduction in assessment by reducing the number of units across AS and A2 by one-third and the amount of coursework at GCSE level.

10.10. In vocational and occupational qualifications, QCA are already seeking ways to reduce the burden of assessment. In particular, they are exploring a range of different forms of moderation of practical assessments, including the use of e-portfolios, which should minimise pressure on students, teachers and trainers. We expect that this will further contribute to reducing the assessment burden.

10.11. We acknowledge that a rigorous examination and assessment system has costs attached. But it is important that a robust system is in place to recognise the achievements of learners.

E-assessment

10.12. In the medium-term, we expect e-assessment to make a significant contribution to cutting the assessment burden and to improving the quality and usage of assessment. Technology can allow learners to take assessments when they are ready and to receive quick and accurate feedback. The KS3 ICT test programme, for example, will offer on-screen practice tests, which are computer marked. Pupils will be able to use them to familiarise themselves with the test environment before taking the formal test. Teachers will be able to use them to assess pupils at any time, as part of assessment for learning. Several awarding bodies also offer on-line tests for a range of subjects, which can be taken by learners at a time that suits them. These developments will relax the constraints of an annual assessment cycle, benefiting both those who are able to progress more quickly and those who need more time to achieve.

10.13. E-assessment can also support our drive to improve functional English and maths. E-assessment is already used for Skills for Life and Key Skills tests. At present the questions are predominantly multiple choice, but we are

---

E-assessment at Unity College

The Unity College school in Northamptonshire participated in a small project to operate a live computer-based examination process. Students took tests in communication, application of number and ICT at levels 1 and 2 with an average 80% pass rate. Pupils were allowed to take e-assessment practice tests in preparation for the real thing.

The comments of pupils were positive:

"I prefer doing it like this than on paper because we are comfortable using computers."

"I got my results straight away rather than waiting…"

"I would be quite happy doing it this way all the time."

ASDAN, the awarding body, reported that "candidates appeared comfortable with taking the tests on the computers, being able to leave when they had finished and with getting results within minutes of taking the test", and that there were no problems in compliance with the test rules.

working with QCA to expand the tests to examine a broader range of skills. We will ask QCA to draw on this experience in developing tests in functional skills as part of GCSE English and maths. This should include ensuring that they are available on-line and on-demand, both to support learning and to allow assessment as soon as the young person is ready.

10.14. Technology also offers the prospect of more innovative assessment that is engaging for learners and draws out their best performance. In vocational qualifications, we should exploit the potential of ICT to develop new mixed methods of assessment. Digital video clips, for example, could be used to show evidence of competence in a workplace and can easily be transmitted for moderation, thus helping to drive up standards and public trust in vocational assessment.

10.15. We will ask QCA to keep e-assessment under continuous review; to exploit its potential wherever possible to improve the quality of assessment and the way it is experienced by students; and to minimise the assessment burden.

Chapter 11
A system configured around young people

Summary

If the changes set out here are to be delivered in practice, we will need to increase the capacity of the education system to offer vocational education. We will do so by building on existing strengths – for example, extending the role of Centres of Vocational Excellence (CoVEs) and other providers in making leading-edge vocational provision available for young people. We will also develop the new Skills Academies as national centres of excellence in skills; and we will strengthen schools' capacity to offer vocational education, through specialism and the new opportunities to take on a second specialism and to become a leading school.

We will also support the workforce to deliver. Demographic changes over the next decade will mean that there are many fewer 14-19 year-olds, which means that delivery of these changes will not require very large numbers of new staff. However, we will ensure that the right staff are in place, including those who have the necessary experience of the workplace to deliver vocational education, and that they have the professional development, qualifications and support that they need to be effective.

Delivery of the full range of curriculum choices to all young people will mean that schools, colleges and other providers in every area will need to work together. A prospectus of options will be made available to all young people, setting out what will be on offer to them in their area. We will ask local authorities and local LSCs to work jointly to draw that up. Where there are any gaps, it will be the responsibility of local authorities and the LSC to commission provision to fill them. Each school and college will be expected to make the full range of choices available to young people on its roll and inspection will ensure that this is the case.

11.1. We have set out an ambitious vision for the 14-19 phase. Ultimately it will be delivered by schools, colleges and other providers, and in particular by the teachers, lecturers, trainers and other staff who work with 14-19 year-olds every day. Our vision represents a significant change summarised in the 'national entitlements' set out overleaf. That change can only happen with the right support from the education infrastructure. The systems for funding and organising schools and colleges and for recruiting and training people to work in them must all contribute to delivering our offer to young people.

We need to evolve from where we are

11.2. The systems that support schools and colleges are effective and well understood by them. We do not see it as desirable or necessary to make wholesale change to the organisation and infrastructure of schools or colleges in England. However, the systems are

National entitlements

Our education system already provides:

- a broad and balanced compulsory curriculum until age 16. Key Stage 4 requires students to study English, maths, science, citizenship, RE and sex education; and to learn about careers and experience work-related and enterprise learning.

- a further entitlement for all 14-16 year-olds to study a modern foreign language, design and technology, a subject from the humanities and one from the arts.

- an entitlement to continue learning until age 18; and

- an entitlement to study functional English, maths and ICT to level 2 until age 19.

We will build on those with new entitlements:

Our new entitlements	When they will start
There will be an entitlement to financial support for young people in learning aged 16-19 who live in low income families	This year
We will create an entitlement to study a science course at Key Stage 4 that will lead to the equivalent of two GCSE qualifications	2006 or as soon as legislation can be passed
We will ensure schools and colleges make all 14 specialised Diplomas available to all young people in every locality	First 8 Diplomas by 2010, all 14 in 2015
We will create an entitlement for all 14-16 year-olds to experience 2 hours of high-quality sport or PE	2010
We will ensure that objective and individualised advice and guidance is available at key points in the 14-19 phase	We will set out our plans in due course
We will introduce an extended project at level 3 and examine how to develop a national entitlement to it	Pilots will begin in 2006

And we will expect all schools and colleges to emulate the best by:

- making functional English and maths their priority, so that all young people who can, achieve level 2 functional skills before they leave learning; and

- tailoring the curriculum to motivate all young people, stretching the brightest and supporting those who are falling behind to catch up.

not perfect and some changes are needed to enable delivery of our offer to young people. It is our intention to work with the grain of existing organisational structures to achieve that change; and to build systems that are driven bottom-up by partnerships of independent, autonomous schools, colleges and training providers.

11.3. The 14-19 system is supported by two main funding streams, with funding for 14-16 year-olds in schools through local authorities and funding for 16-19 year-olds through the LSC. An effective system depends on stable funding. After the difficulties for some schools' funding in 2003, we have taken steps to guarantee funding stability for schools and have now published a consultation document on proposals to simplify the school funding system from 2006. We will provide schools with 3-year budgets and make it easier for them to plan in the longer term. The LSC has also made funding provision for young people its highest priority and is reviewing how to direct more of its resources to front line provision.

11.4. There is also record capital investment in schools through 'Building Schools for the Future' and in colleges through the LSC's capital investment programme. The potential of this investment for 14-19 reform is not only improved facilities, supporting high quality vocational education, but the chance for real transformation area by area.

Existing barriers must be overcome to enable the system to work in young people's best interests

11.5. Our vision for the 14-19 phase sets out a range of opportunities that should be available to young people in every area of the country. Schools, colleges and training providers will need to collaborate, because no single institution will be able to provide them all on its own. We need to remove barriers and disincentives to collaboration in the education system:

- In the past, there has been no expectation that schools and colleges might buy from other providers in order to increase quality or breadth. If we are to take advantage of existing specialist staff and facilities, that will need to change.

- The systems exist for institutions to purchase places on courses from other providers, but there is a visible marginal cost. A school sending a few learners to study at college will have to pay for their course places, but will not see a reduction in its requirements for staff and facilities.

- There are 'start-up' costs to collaborative working. Institutions working together to meet the needs of young people in an area will need to analyse what provision is needed, agree which institutions will deliver it and organise it so that all young people in the area can access it.

- There are substantial logistical challenges to collaboration to enable young people to learn at more than one institution at the same time. For example, schools and colleges will need to co-ordinate their timetables and arrange transport between them.

11.6. In overcoming these challenges, we will build on the substantial successful experience from the 300 local partnerships involved in the Increased Flexibility Programme (IFP). These partnerships of schools, colleges and training providers have been developed to deliver a wider range of vocational qualifications for 14-16 year olds. They provide the opportunity to study off-site at a college or with a training provider for one or two days a week throughout Key Stage 4. Partnerships have typically received £100,000 a year to support collaboration and over 90,000 young people have benefited from a broader range of opportunities.

The Increased Flexibility Programme in Basingstoke

Tutors from Basingstoke College of Technology (BCOT) are providing vocational courses in local schools as part of the Increased Flexibility Programme. Currently over 700 students in years 10 and 11 are following vocational courses; and teachers in the schools are also developing the expertise to deliver the courses themselves.

The college tutors are able to share good practice on delivery methods, styles of teaching and a range of resources; they are supporting teachers to develop their understanding of the standard of work required for each grade band. College staff also bring a range of recent industry experience.

Daniel Bosley who is 16 is now studying full-time at BCOT for a BTEC First Diploma in Sound Engineering. Previously he took a Certificate in Sound Engineering alongside a range of GCSEs at Costello Technology College. "Because BCOT worked with my school I was able to get an understanding of the wide range of career opportunities in engineering and of what would be involved in an engineering course. I felt far more confident in starting this course here at BCOT. Quite a few students here have enrolled after being able to study these vocational courses while still at school."

We will build the capacity in the system to deliver the new entitlement

11.7. We need to be sure that there is the capacity in every part of the country to deliver a range of quality vocational programmes to 14-19 year-olds. In many places only limited vocational options are available from age 14. We need to increase the amount of vocational provision that is available.

We will ensure that there is sufficient provision on offer

11.8. We want schools, colleges and training providers in each area to decide together how they will deliver the full range of 14-19 options. Each institution should be able to play to its strengths, including specialist vocational or academic options of interest to relatively small numbers of learners in the area. Some institutions, such as leading schools or Centres of Vocational Excellence (CoVEs) will have a particularly important role to play. Local authorities and local LSCs will be responsible for ensuring that sufficient provision is available to meet the needs of young people and employers.

11.9. Young people will continue to be based in a school until age 16, but may spend up to 2 days a week in other settings. Each learner's 'home' institution will be responsible for securing the provision they need, and for pastoral support. For 14-16 year-olds, we expect schools to be responsible for purchasing provision from others, but also to be enhancing their own vocational provision. The specialist schools programme will help to develop schools' capacity to offer vocational education. We will expect every specialist school to offer applied learning in the area of its specialism. They should set out what they will offer on applying for specialist status, and at redesignation. Over the next 5 years virtually all schools will achieve specialist status.

11.10. Last year we announced that the very best Specialist Schools would be able to become leading schools, taking on a new role in driving change through the school system. One of the roles will be to boost vocational provision in an area. To reflect its importance, this option will attract an additional £30,000 of funding on top of the £60 per pupil payable for second specialism. The leading school might develop new provision itself for its own pupils and for others, or it might work through others to do so. The leading school and its partners should share their developing expertise with others locally.

11.11. Which institution provides what will be decided locally on the basis of quality. We expect schools to play an increasing role in providing vocational education. Nonetheless, the role of CoVEs and colleges will be of particular importance. Colleges contain the largest number of teaching staff with skills and experience in vocational education and the up-to-date technical facilities that are needed for delivery in many vocational courses. We should therefore look to colleges which meet the standard to provide vocational leadership for the whole system, including curriculum development and sharing the expertise of advanced skills practitioners as well as facilities.

11.12. Colleges will therefore provide vocational opportunities to increasing numbers of 14-16 year-olds. Colleges will also be the major providers of level 3 vocational pathways for 16-19 year-olds. They will need to plan this in collaboration with other providers. Sir Andrew Foster's review of FE colleges will be significant here. In addition, we set out in our 5-year strategy our plans to allow more schools to engage in post-16 provision. That will also be important in increasing the capacity of the system to deliver our vision, and we will consult shortly on the details.

11.13. Many schools in each area are working increasingly with local colleges to share facilities and expertise, as part of the specialist schools programme or in other ways. We will continue to support these developments to grow towards a network of high quality facilities with leading and Specialist Schools in each area linked with colleges and CoVEs providing centres of expertise at national, regional and local level. The network will also be supported by new national Skills Academies. Our longer-term aim is to have at least one Skills Academy for each vocational area, closely linked to the relevant SSC and directly to employers. Further detail on these Skills Academies will be set out in the forthcoming Skills White Paper.

11.14. Successful partnership working takes time and effort to establish. Its success depends on:

- a group of confident, independent institutions choosing to work together towards a shared aim;

- a clear articulation of that aim, which must be focused on the needs of young people in the area;

- each institution being clear about what its strengths can contribute to the partnership and how it can draw on the strengths of others;

- commitment to mutual accountability for the delivery of outcomes; and

- a joint agreement identifying responsibilities and funding at partnership and institution level.

11.15. We will shortly be publishing a prospectus and web-based advice on effective practice through Education Improvement Partnerships. These will enable schools and other institutions to collaborate to raise standards and work together to take on wider responsibilities for service delivery for children and young people on behalf of the local authority. We expect that Education Improvement Partnerships will provide a vehicle for the delivery of 14-19 collaboration where no effective partnership currently exists; and that existing partnerships will evolve to take on wider responsibilities.

We will raise the quality of provision

11.16. Only a few institutions currently provide good vocational options to learners throughout the 14-19 phase. Schools with only limited experience of offering vocational options and colleges that mainly cater to over-16s will need support:

- We will set up new sector-based Skills Academies to act as national centres of excellence in each sector and to drive quality through the system. Skills Academies will focus on the needs of the post-16 sector and will be supported by a regional and sectoral network of CoVEs.

- We will ask the Specialist Schools Trust to provide support for leading and Specialist Schools in vocational education. They will work with other expert bodies and draw on the experience of schools that already make high quality vocational provision including through involvement with the

Increased Flexibility Programme or 14-19 pathfinders.

- The New Relationship with Schools will provide a powerful lever to help schools to tackle areas of underperformance. Colleges are held to account against 3-year development plans agreed with the LSC and must meet national minimum standards. We will intervene decisively where schools and colleges are unable to address persistent problems.

11.17. We will set up a national quality improvement body for the post-16 sector from April 2006, to be known as the Quality Improvement Agency for Lifelong Learning (QuILL). First announced in November 2004, this agency will secure better outcomes for learners, employers, communities and the economy by providing a national focus on quality improvement in the sector. The agency will make specific contributions to 14-19 provision:

- Building on the programme managed by our Standards Unit, the agency will commission support materials and services to help providers drive up quality and respond to employer and learner needs.

- It will oversee a network of advisers who will produce tailored packages of support to address the needs of providers. It will support School Improvement Partners to advise on improvement in schools with sixth forms or making vocational provision.

- It will co-ordinate and support effective transfer of good practice and innovation in vocational provision, working with Skills Academies, CoVEs and others.

We will support the workforce to deliver

11.18. We need the right people with the right skills to teach young people in schools, colleges and training providers. Teachers,

tutors, teaching assistants, secondees from industry and a range of other people are crucial to delivering the 14-19 phase. The skill mix in that workforce will need to change as more learners take vocational options.

Overall numbers

11.19. By far the most important driver of any change in the total number of staff needed in schools and colleges as a result of our proposals will be the number of 16-19 year-olds participating in post-compulsory education. At present 75% of 17 year-olds participate in learning. Over the next 10 years as we implement our reforms, we want this to increase to over 90%. However, the number of 16-19 year-olds in England will fall sharply over that period, so even such a dramatic rise in participation will cause only a very small change in the actual number of 16-19 year-olds in learning.

11.20. Staffing numbers in the education system are at record levels and have risen significantly due to investment since 1997.

Secondary school teachers (FTE)[3]	211,000
Secondary school support staff:	81,000[4] – including
• teaching assistants	25,000
• technicians	18,000
• administration staff	27,000
• other education support staff eg learning mentors and welfare assistants	10,000
College teachers (FTE)	75,000
College support staff (FTE)	75,000
Staff in work-based learning providers	60,000
Connexions Personal Advisers	8,000[5]

Sources: LSC Staff Statistics, 2002/03, www.lsc.gov.uk; DfES Statistical First Release Statistics of Education: School Workforce in England (2004); Nexus – Connexions Partnership Management Information; LLUK calculations.

11.21. We do not expect these reforms to require more teaching staff in schools. Most of

[3] Full-time equivalents.
[4] We are seeking to expand considerably on this number as part of the workforce remodelling agenda.
[5] Overall number. Many Connexions Personal Advisers are based in secondary schools.

the increase in post-16 participation will be in vocational courses, largely provided by FE colleges and training providers. Increasing numbers of 14-16 year-olds studying vocational courses will spend part of their time in colleges rather than school.

11.22. The demand for extra vocational courses in FE colleges will largely be offset by the fall in the number of 14-19 year-olds in England. However, there will need to be additional staff to deliver the types of courses we want to offer these learners. We will bring more specialist professionals with relevant expertise from business into colleges and training providers. The new 'passport to teaching' module being developed as part of the Success for All reforms will be available to equip them with the skills and knowledge required to teach.

11.23. The total increases in staff numbers in schools and colleges needed to implement our reforms will be of the order of:

- 1,250-1,450 support staff in schools and colleges to help manage collaborative arrangements and provide teaching and learning support; and

- 1,000-1,250 college staff in teaching roles, mainly made up of people with relevant specialist business experience.

11.24. We will carefully monitor the effects of each change we make to the 14-19 phase to ensure that there are enough staff with the right skills in schools, colleges and training providers to deliver the 14-19 offer and that schools and colleges are able to manage them flexibly to do so.

A workforce with the right skills to deliver

11.25. The changes we are introducing provide new challenges but also offer new opportunities to teachers. A number of changes will be important to the workforce:

- Offering a new range of tests for teacher assessment at Key Stage 3. We want to support teachers to make best use of the national bank of tests.

- Introducing the extended project. Teachers will help learners select their project; they will monitor and guide learners' progress.

- The QCA review of the Key Stage 3 curriculum will lead to changes in the programmes of study. Changes to some GCSEs will have implications for how they are taught. We will provide CPD and support teachers through the Secondary National Strategy.

- Introducing new qualifications, including the new Diplomas. We will support teachers and trainers to deliver these courses and assess parts of them.

11.26. We are confident that with the right support teachers, FE lecturers, trainers and support staff will be able to adapt to these changes. We will work with the Teacher Training Agency, the Institute for Learning, Lifelong Learning UK and other key partners to develop high quality training and development for teaching staff. In September 2004, we announced that from 2007-8 we would invest an additional £70 million in workforce development for the post-16 sector, including £30 million for initial teacher training.

11.27. As part of 'Success for All' we are investing some £14.4 million through 2003-6 to support the Centre for Excellence in Leadership to improve leadership and management skills in the post-16 sector. As a result, we expect to see better leadership, greater diversity and better progression of staff into leadership posts.

11.28. We will also task the National College for School Leadership and the Centre for Excellence in Leadership to work together on leadership development and support to equip head teachers, FE principals and work-based learning providers to work effectively in

Using professional expertise to engage students, improve teaching and serve the local economy in the Lake District

South Lakeland is dominated by the hospitality and tourism industry, but labour market intelligence and local hotels and catering outlets reported staff shortages. A radical approach was needed.

Kendal College appointed a chef to work with four secondary schools in the area to raise the profile of catering and bring the learning experience to life. Simon Hansen, a two rosette award winner, works with GCSE catering students and runs an after-school Junior Chef Club for 14 year-olds. Teaching staff are also benefiting from Simon's expertise and have taken the opportunity to update their own skills.

Interest has spread rapidly to other schools and demand to get on courses is growing. Students and teachers are delighted to be learning skills from a professional. The Junior Chef Club has proved so popular that there are now two sessions and many more students are considering a career in hospitality and tourism.

collaboration and ensure that all their staff are trained in the skills they need.

High quality teaching and learning materials

11.29. Building capacity in the system needs high quality teaching and learning materials. We will support the development of Diploma programmes with new teaching and learning materials informed by the needs of employers and SSCs, through the transformation programme which is managed by the Department's Standards Unit. Resources include teaching materials such as lesson plans, activities for learners and CPD materials for teachers, trainers, tutors and assessors. These materials will be available on the National Learning Network. From April 2006, the new Quality Improvement Agency for Lifelong Learning will be responsible for this transformation programme.

11.30. E-learning and the broader use of learning technologies have the potential to transform the way skills are developed and skills training delivered, both in the workplace and elsewhere. It will be important to develop e-learning that supports integration between learning in the classroom and the workplace. To facilitate this, the Department has supported the appointment of an e-learning champion for the Skills for Business Network, based at e-skills UK, to provide expert support for SSCs on the potential of e-learning.

We will ensure that the full range of options is available in each area

11.31. This White Paper describes our vision of a reformed 14-19 phase. As we begin to implement the changes to the curriculum and qualifications for 14-19 year-olds, we will set out national standards for delivery. These will include a clear statement of the choices that should be available to meet the needs of all young people in every area of the country.

11.32. We know that schools and colleges are most effective when they have the autonomy to innovate and adapt to their local circumstances. But autonomy is not a barrier to effective partnership. We want institutions in each locality to work together to decide how best to deliver the 14-19 offer, with each institution able to play to its strengths. To support them we will provide a range of examples, drawing on the experience of the 14-19 pathfinders and IFP that show how this can be done well. We will provide advice to help institutions that want to contract provision from each other or to enter into shared staffing or governance arrangements. We will legislate to increase the scope for joint governance arrangements between schools and FE colleges to strengthen collaborative activity.

11.33. We want the system to be driven bottom-up by partnerships of schools, colleges and other providers who together decide how they are best placed to make a comprehensive offer to young people. But there is also an important role for local authorities and local LSCs to facilitate and enable this planning and to challenge partners if there are gaps in provision. There is already substantial experience of this being done well, for example in joint action planning in response to 14-19 area inspections. We envisage a similar process enabling and incentivising the wider collaboration that will be needed to deliver our vision of a system that will meet the needs of all young people in every area.

11.34. We think the steps in the process should be:

- Schools, colleges and other providers set out what they propose to offer both individually and collaboratively, on what scale and to which students.

- The local authority and the local LSC draw together this information to identify any gaps against the national standards, or barriers to effective collaboration.

- The LSC would hold a flexible funding pot (as it does now with the pathfinders and IFP), which would be used to commission additional provision and provide some additional funding for transport and partnership management, to ensure that the national standards are met for all young people in the area.

- The end product is a prospectus, jointly published by the local authority and the local LSC for all the providers, which sets out for each young person a clear picture of what is available in the area.

11.35. The prospectus should be made available to all young people in the area. We will publish the prospectuses for every area in the country on a single website. Each prospectus will be the basis for independent advice and guidance to young people about the options available to them.

11.36. The aim of this model is to put learners in the driving seat, able to make informed choices between institutions and about whether to take advantage of another provider's offer. This depends on each institution actively contributing to making the local offer available to all young people and working towards their success at age 19, and on effective facilitation by the LSC or local authority.

11.37. Our proposals for changes to the accountability framework will encourage institutions to do this. Performance tables that recognise a wider range of qualifications and focus on the value added to learners are an incentive to provide a curriculum and qualifications offer which makes it more likely that young people will succeed. Once the offer is available in each area, the inspection framework can assess whether schools and colleges are making the best use of the opportunities available to young people.

We will continue to keep the delivery system under review

11.38. We know that schools and colleges are committed to the success of the young people they teach. Delivering the 14-19 offer will contribute to that success for greater numbers of young people. This is something that institutions will want to do. In this Chapter we have described a clear set of mechanisms that will enable them to make the offer available to all young people in the country. We know that effective collaboration to deliver the 14-19 offer is possible, because it is already happening in 14-19 pathfinder projects and other schools and colleges. We will ensure that the lessons of that experience are shared.

11.39. Nonetheless, our proposals will require a major change to the way 14-19 learning is delivered in most parts of the country. We want to examine in detail the ways that this can work best. It is particularly important that the funding system supports delivery of the 14-19 offer, as it is implemented in full over the next 10 years. We will therefore keep progress with this system under review.

Successful partnership in Knowsley

The Knowsley 14-19 Collegiate aims to create a new flexible single phase of education that will enable young people to learn and achieve in ways best suited to their individual needs.

The Collegiate has six formal partners, each of whom has committed to the collegiate principle and is represented within its decision making structure through the Executive Group. The partners are: Knowsley local authority, the local LSC, the secondary and special schools, Knowsley Community College, Connexions, and Jaguar. The governance and management structure of the partnership comprises a Governance Forum, an Executive Group and an Operations Group. The Collegiate has enabled 650 students to take courses in the new Vocational Skills Centre and at Knowsley Community College. A local authority-wide KS4 prospectus has been produced giving details of each of the courses. One of the new GCSEs in vocational subjects is to be provided jointly with Jaguar, while another is taught jointly by a school, a college and a training provider. All schools have agreed to timetable one year 10 option on a Wednesday afternoon, and in some cases there has been further co-ordination of timetables. Knowsley is the first 14-19 area inspection area to receive an 'outstanding' grade for effective and efficient provision that meets the needs of learners, employers and the community.

We will ensure that the supporting system is in place

11.40. We will work closely with the QCA, the National Assessment Agency (NAA) and awarding bodies to develop Diplomas and make the proposed changes to existing qualifications. The awarding bodies have an important role to play. While we want SSCs, employers and universities to play a key role in designing the outcomes of each Diploma, it is the awarding bodies who will draw on their expertise to turn these specifications into deliverable programmes, syllabuses and assessment criteria.

11.41. Changes to the qualifications system on this scale will need to be carefully managed and introduced without additional administrative burdens. NAA will continue to work with awarding bodies to build on the reforms delivered through the exams modernisation programme for general qualifications, for example bringing together their administrative processes. Additionally, we will ask QCA and the awarding bodies to develop an agreed set of principles that should underpin awarding bodies' work. These might include:

- focusing on the needs of learners;

- maintaining and improving public confidence in standards;

- reducing costs and bureaucratic burdens on schools, colleges and other providers, in particular through developing common systems; and

- actively consulting with employers, HE and subject bodies.

11.42. We will ask QCA to keep the development of the qualifications system under review to ensure that it is fit for purpose and efficient, and to advise us on whether any regulatory or legislative changes might be necessary in future.

Chapter 12
A sharp accountability framework, which makes sure that we offer the best to young people

Summary

We need an accountability framework which supports and encourages the development of the 14-19 phase we want.

We will therefore incentivise institutions to offer the full range of specialised lines to their students by including these qualifications in the performance tables and ensuring that as the new vocational arrangements are put in place, inspections ask searching questions about the curriculum and qualifications being made available.

We will incentivise focus on the basics through continuing to publish Key Stage 3 Achievement and Attainment Tables in English, maths and science; and through changing tables at 16 to focus on 5 A*-C GCSEs including English and maths.

We will incentivise stretch for all young people through the New Relationship with Schools, which will mean that schools are held to account for the progress of all their students; and through ensuring that schools are given credit in the performance tables when young people achieve success in higher level qualifications.

We will incentivise progression by developing progression targets; and through ensuring that the achievement of young people completing Key Stage 4 later than the normal age is properly credited to their home institution. And we will ensure that all learners have their achievements recognised in the tables.

12.1. A new 14-19 phase which enables all young people to fulfil their potential will depend on a sharper, more discriminating accountability framework for schools, colleges and training providers.

12.2. Institutions are primarily responsible for their performance and quality, but they should be held publicly accountable for their achievements. An open and transparent accountability framework helps institutions to maintain and raise standards; provides information to enable the inspectorates, local authorities and the LSC to challenge and support institutions; and helps parents and young people make choices about the opportunities available to them. In this White Paper we have set out a vision for a 14-19 phase in which all young people should achieve their full potential. The accountability framework and the informed choices of learners should together mobilise and motivate institutions to deliver that vision.

12.3. We have already developed a robust and sensitive accountability framework for schools, colleges and training providers which has been very effective in maintaining and improving their performance. In the light of that success, we are making a small number of changes to the accountability framework to ensure that it supports the key elements of our vision for the

14-19 phase and continues the move towards a common approach to accountability and measures of success for all institutions. The accountability framework can help to ensure that:

- schools make sure that 14 year-olds have secure functional skills and are ready for a range of options;

- functional skills are prioritised throughout the 14-19 phase;

- institutions encourage young people to progress as soon as they are able;

- institutions encourage a culture of staying on and achieving worthwhile qualifications until 19;

- the achievements of all young people are recognised, promoting equality of opportunity, regardless of background; and

- all institutions, including 11-16 schools, work towards these goals.

12.4. It will be important to keep a close eye on how our system performs in comparison to other countries. We are participating in OECD work to develop indicators which give us the most rigorous comparisons of our educational performance and participation with other countries.

Uses the full balance of accountability measures

12.5. An intelligent accountability framework that seeks to incentivise all these behaviours and outcomes will need to use a range of different levers. The main levers work in different ways:

- Tests measure the attainment of young people at a specific moment in their learning, usually at the end of a particular phase of learning.

- Achievement and Attainment Tables and school profiles aggregate the test results of a year-group of learners to give a measure of the success of the institutions teaching them.

- Targets are set for individual learners, institutions, groups of institutions and bodies like local authorities and local LSCs.

- Inspection provides a detailed and expert appraisal of how well a provider is meeting the needs of its learners, or the performance of institutions across a whole geographic area.

- Performance management allows teachers and tutors to agree objectives, including for professional development, aligned with the priorities of their institution.

Key components of the existing accountability framework

Tests	At 14: External tests in English, maths, science and, from 2008, ICT From 16-19: External qualifications in most subjects studied
Tables	The School and College Achievement and Attainment Tables report **At age 14:** • the percentage of pupils achieving level 5 in English, maths, science, and from 2008, ICT; and • value added from Key Stage 2 to 3. **At age 16:** • the percentage of learners achieving level 2, ie 5 or more A*-C GCSE or equivalent; • the percentage of learners achieving level 1, ie 5 or more A*-G GCSE or equivalent; • the percentage of learners achieving at least one entry level qualification; and • value added from Key Stage 2 to 4 and from Key Stage 3 to 4. **At age 18:** • average A level (or equivalent) point score per student; • average point score per examination; and • from 2006, value added at level 3. We separately publish learner outcomes in FE colleges and work-based learning, including a measure of the number of young people achieving level 2 and level 3 by age 19. Detailed benchmarking data on Success, Retention and Achievement Rates in FE Colleges is published by the LSC.
Targets and plans	Schools set targets for: • achievement at Key Stage 3 (statutory target); and • achievement at age 16 (statutory target). Schools will produce their Development Plans with the support and challenge of a School Improvement Partner – an experienced education professional. They will identify priority areas for improvement and set targets to do so. FE colleges must set improvement targets in their three-year development plans and agree them with the LSC. A proportion of their funding is conditional on setting and meeting those targets. FE colleges and training providers must set targets for learner success rates. They must meet national floor targets by 2006. Colleges must also set improvement targets for the level of employer engagement in their provision.

National PSA targets to increase the proportion of young people achieving level 2 and level 3 define the goals for each part of the education system. We have set targets to:

- increase the proportion of 19 year-olds who achieve at least level 2 by 3 percentage points between 2004 and 2006;

- increase that number by a further 2 percentage points between 2006 and 2008; and

- increase the proportion of young people who achieve level 3.

Inspection

New inspection arrangements are being introduced in schools and colleges from September 2005. These will focus more on evidence from self-evaluation and the robustness of the institution's management. The overall burden of inspection will be cut, and notice periods for schools shortened. However, inspections will be more frequent in weak institutions.

Making sure that 14 year-olds have secure functional skills and are ready for a range of pathways

12.6. The accountability system for schools needs to emphasise the importance of achievement at age 14. Good functional skills and a knowledge of English, maths, science and ICT will be essential for learners to access the 14-19 phase. The learning they have undertaken in the other National Curriculum subjects will provide a sound basis for further learning post-14 and for making choices between subjects.

12.7. The School and College Achievement and Attainment Tables already report pupils' achievements at age 14 in English, maths and science. When the KS3 ICT test is introduced in 2008, we will include ICT results in the Tables and require schools to set targets for those results.

12.8. Schools should also report to parents how well their pupils achieve in the foundation subjects and whether they have acquired the learning skills needed to access the range of pathways from 14-19. Each young person will receive a Pupil Profile showing their performance in all the KS3 subjects. This should include the overall results for the school, the local authority and nationally, so that parents can see how their child compares to his or her peers and how well the school is doing.

12.9. Schools should include their KS3 results in their school profile, which will be available on-line, so that current and prospective parents can see how well the school prepares its pupils for the 14-19 phase of learning. English, maths, science and, from 2008, ICT results from national tests will be included automatically. Schools will be expected to report on progress across KS3 drawing on the results of teacher assessment.

Prioritising functional skills throughout the 14-19 phase

12.10. Strong functional skills in English, maths and ICT are essential at every stage of learning, for employment, to be able to engage in society and enjoy adult life. We expect the vast majority of learners to achieve National Curriculum level 5 in the functional skills at 14, and to achieve functional skills to at least level 2 on the National Qualifications Framework at 16 (equivalent to C or better at GCSE). The accountability framework is a crucial lever for intensifying the focus on these essentials at every stage of learning.

12.11. At age 16, the most widely recognised measure of success for schools is how many of their students achieve level 2 (5 A*-C grades in GCSE and equivalent qualifications).

We will change this measure to prioritise English and maths at level 2. The new measure in the Tables will be the number of students achieving Diploma standard – ie 5 A*-C grades (or equivalent) including English and maths. This measure will incentivise schools to make sure that young people have the functional skills, as well as the breadth of learning, needed to study until 19.

Accountability system to promote progression

12.12. The accountability framework should promote engaging, enjoyable and stretching learning programmes for all young people. Young people should be encouraged to progress to higher levels of study as soon as they are able.

12.13. The accountability system should incentivise progression and respond to the fact that some young people will be ready for qualifications before the usual age, while others may need longer to prepare if they are to fulfil their potential. We have already made a number of changes to the Achievement and Attainment Tables to support this and we want to build on these.

12.14. Where young people complete their GCSEs before they are 16, their results are 'banked' and counted in their school or college results for their year group. The institution does not lose out in the Tables by entering young people before age 16. Following a pilot last year, from 2005 the Tables will report learners' achievements when they finish KS4, rather than at the end of compulsory schooling. That means the results of pupils will be reported whether they are younger or older than 16 when they complete KS4. We will also report their KS3 results when they take the last of the 3 tests in English, maths and science. This is similar to the method already used for post-16 results: these are reported when the pupil completes two years of advanced study, whether that is at age 17, 18 or 19.

12.15. Young people who achieve AS levels by age 16 are already counted against their institution's performance in the KS4 Tables. A good grade at AS level is worth more than an A* GCSE in the institution's overall results, thereby rewarding it for encouraging the brightest learners to progress to AS level early. We also want to encourage young people who excel post-16 to move on to studying HE modules. We will explore with the QCA whether these could be recognised in the post-16 Tables.

Encourage a culture of staying on and achieving worthwhile qualifications until 19

12.16. All young people should be able to fulfil their potential and achieve at age 19. The accountability framework needs to prioritise achievement at that age and to recognise the wide range of different qualifications that young people will be following. All institutions, whether or not they teach to age 19, should regard contributing to the success of young people at that age as their main aim.

12.17. The accountability framework ought to encourage institutions teaching 11-16 year olds to take responsibility for their future progression and success after the end of compulsory education. Schools, colleges and training providers should ensure that all young people achieve to the best of their ability, are engaged in learning and well advised about their future options.

12.18. We will record what qualifications the year 11 pupils from each school go on to achieve by age 19, wherever they choose to study. We will use this data to develop a progression measure, to show how successful the pupils of each school are in gaining qualifications after leaving age. This measure can be used to set targets to improve progression.

12.19. The Connexions Service also collects a wider set of information about young people's destinations, including whether they go on to university or into employment. We will continue to develop this data source and make it available to local LSCs, local authorities and the inspectorates to inform the planning and accountability of provision in each locality.

12.20. The Achievement and Attainment Tables already include value-added measures for 11-16 institutions, which show how far learners have progressed since entering secondary school. We are developing a range of similar measures for post-16 learning, to incentivise institutions to ensure that all young people who stay on in learning continue to progress. These include:

- A measure of value-added for 16-19 learners following level 3 qualifications. An institutional value added measure will be introduced in the Achievement and Attainment Tables in 2006, after a pilot this year.

- A complementary measure of distance travelled for 16-19 learners, which is being developed by the LSC and the Inspectorates. This will measure learner progress on qualifications at level 1 and 2 and ungraded qualifications like NVQs at all levels.

- A measure of qualifications achieved by learners as a proportion of the qualifications they start. This qualification success measure is already in use in colleges. Changes to the PLASC survey will mean that this measure can be applied in school sixth forms from around 2008. From September 2005, the qualification success measure used in training providers will be brought into line with the measure used in colleges.

12.21. Schools, colleges and training providers will be able to access detailed value-added and distance-travelled information through the Learner Achievement Tracker which will be piloted from September 2005. The Learner Achievement Tracker will enable institutions to compare the progress of their learners with national norms, for the majority of qualifications and subjects they provide for 16-19 year-olds.

Recognition of the achievements of all young people

12.22. We want all young people to achieve their full potential throughout the 14-19 phase. This means that every young person should be stretched to achieve their best, and that achievement should be recognised. Value added and distance travelled measures show how far learners have progressed compared to the national average. Institutions which enable all learners to progress as far as they can, from whatever starting point, will get better value added and distance travelled scores.

12.23. Our proposals for a New Relationship with Schools will help to ensure that all groups of pupils are being stretched. Schools will have access to powerful value-added data to show how different groups of their pupils progress. They will evaluate how to tackle the problems facing any underperforming groups, with the support of an expert School Improvement Partner (SIP). SIPs will be able to identify patterns in performance and challenge schools on the progress of different groups of children, for example the lowest- or highest-achieving 20%, or children from particular ethnic minorities, on the basis of high quality benchmarked information.

12.24. We will expect schools to describe in their school profile how they are improving standards for all learners. They should set out what action they have taken to support young people, for example, with SEN or who are gifted or talented. We will be encouraging better assessment approaches for such pupils enabling schools to personalise the learning and be more ambitious for the standards achieved by pupils of different abilities.

12.25. We already include all approved qualifications in the Achievement and Attainment Tables, to recognise the achievements of all young people. The Tables will continue to recognise new, high quality qualifications that are developed so as to encourage schools and colleges to offer young people a wide range of pathways. We will ensure that the Tables give proper recognition to the achievement of a full Diploma, attaching more weight to that than achieving a mix of unrelated vocational qualifications.

12.26. Although we expect most learners to reach level 2, achievements of other learners also deserve recognition. The Tables already include a measure of the number of learners achieving level 1 or entry level qualifications at 16. These measures, together with the measures of progression post-16 that we are developing, signal that we will recognise the achievements of all young people by age 19.

All institutions, including 11-16 schools, to work towards these goals

12.27. A more varied and flexible 14-19 phase will mean that many young people are taught in more than one institution at the same time. Learners will face more choices about where and what to study at age 14 and 16. The accountability framework will incentivise each institution to provide the best quality teaching and contribute to the success of each learner. We also want to use accountability levers to ensure that the choice of provision available in each locality meets the needs of all its learners.

12.28. Ofsted and other inspectorates will introduce Joint Area Reviews from September 2005 to assess how well services work together to improve the lives of children and young people. They will report on whether the choices available can support progression to further and higher education, training and employment for all learners. These reviews and the inspections of individual institutions will analyse both the quality of learning opportunities available and the reliability of the information, guidance and support offered to young people.

12.29. We will work with Ofsted and ALI to ensure that the inspection arrangements for areas and for individual institutions continue to reflect the changes to the 14-19 phase and remain fit for purpose.

Chapter 13
Delivering the new 14-19 phase

13.1. We are embarking on a significant programme of change. Some of the changes can be introduced quickly. Others will take much longer. We will produce a full timetable in due course, but the outline below sets out our timetable for the major changes.

2005

- More GCSEs in vocational subjects

- More Young Apprenticeships

- Roll-out enterprise education

- Pilot English and maths GCSE changes

- Agreement on Diploma lines

- Establish first Skills Academies

- First vocational leading schools announced

2006

- A level differentiation data to HEIs

- Extended project pilot

- New science KS4 and GCSEs

- Upgrade CoVE network

2007

- Legislation to free up local governance

- Start of major CPD for school and college staff

2008

- KS3 curriculum and assessment changes

- First four Diploma lines available

- 12 Skills Academies open

- 200 vocational leading schools in place

2010

- All vocational lines available

- Eight Diploma lines a nationwide entitlement

- Further 13 Skills Academies

2015

- All Diplomas a nationwide entitlement

13.2. We have published alongside this document a Regulatory Impact Asessment, setting out some more detail of likely organisational effects over time. This is available on the DfES website. We will design specialised Diplomas, learning from successful qualification systems in other countries. We will make sure that reforms are compatible with arrangements in other countries as far as possible.

Printed in the UK for The Stationery Office Limited
on behalf of the Controller of Her Majesty's Stationery Office
02/05,176940